T0339687

Campfire Lessons for Leaders

This ideal companion for business leaders heading into a milestone moment offers practical advice to help them take something that can seem amorphous and abstract – living an intentional, purposeful life – and turn it into reality.

Though it might seem counterintuitive, this book demonstrates that to move forward in the right direction, you must understand and integrate your past into your present. Readers will see how they too can step back and consider the "flashpoints" of their past in a way that will serve them as they take the next step of their life, from navigating a significant life change to simply living each day feeling less stuck and more purposeful. Leading coach Tony Martignetti shares the most powerful lessons from over 200 "Virtual Campfire" podcast interviews he's conducted with driven individuals who decided to live intentionally rather than by default. As no two interviewees have faced the same challenges or pursued the same goals, readers will be inspired by these diverse insights to embark on – and sustain – their own unique transformations.

Packed with questions, journaling prompts, and real-world exercises to help readers understand their past at a deeper level and integrate it into their present, this book provides a valuable toolkit for business leaders and professionals in any industry who feel unfulfilled and uncertain about what's next for them.

Tony Martignetti, Chief Inspiration Officer at Inspired Purpose Partners, is a trusted advisor, leadership coach and facilitator, best-selling author, podcast host, and speaker. He brings together over 25 years of business and leadership experience and extreme curiosity to elevate leaders and equip them with the tools to navigate through change and unlock their true potential. Find out more about Tony at www.ipurposepartners.com.

Campfire Lessons for Leaders

How Uncovering Our Past Can Propel Us Forward

Tony Martignetti

Routledge
Taylor & Francis Group

NEW YORK AND LONDON

Designed cover image: Getty

First published 2024
by Routledge
605 Third Avenue, New York, NY 10158

and by Routledge
4 Park Square, Milton Park, Abingdon, Oxon, OX14 4RN

Routledge is an imprint of the Taylor & Francis Group, an informa business

© 2024 Tony Martignetti

Library of Congress Cataloguing-in-Publication Data
Names: Martignetti, Tony, author.
Title: Campfire lessons for leaders : how uncovering our past can propel us forward / Tony Martignetti.
Description: New York, NY : Routledge, 2024. |
Identifiers: LCCN 2023032105 (print) | LCCN 2023032106 (ebook) |
ISBN 9781032429021 (hardback) | ISBN 9781032428994 (paperback) |
ISBN 9781003364818 (ebook)
Subjects: LCSH: Leadership.
Classification: LCC HD57.7 .M392458 2024 (print) | LCC HD57.7 (ebook) | DDC 658.4/092--dc23/eng/20230713
LC record available at https://lccn.loc.gov/2023032105
LC ebook record available at https://lccn.loc.gov/2023032106

ISBN: 978-1-032-42902-1 (hbk)
ISBN: 978-1-032-42899-4 (pbk)
ISBN: 978-1-003-36481-8 (ebk)

DOI: 10.4324/9781003364818

Typeset in Times New Roman
by MPS Limited, Dehradun

For my wife, Lauri, and my son, Aiden. Your patience and understanding have made this and so many other things possible.

Contents

Acknowledgments

"Acknowledging the good that you already have in your life is the foundation for all abundance." – *Eckhart Tolle*

As we let the embers burn out on our campfire, I want to take this opportunity to show my appreciation for my fellow campers. Writing this book has been a journey through an uncharted wilderness, and I did not traverse the trails alone. I could not have written this book without a team of supporters, editors, well-wishers, and, of course, my incredible guests.

Before you move on to forge a path in your life, please join me in acknowledging this hearty band of trailblazers who have been instrumental in turning this book from a spark of an idea into a roaring, inspirational bonfire. Without them, we might still be fumbling with the matches!

In no particular order: Lora Denton, Dolores Hirschmann, Ken Lizotte, Elena Petricone, Dorie Clark, Rob Salafia, Hal Gregersen, Peter Bregman, Whitney Johnson, Todd Cherches, Nancy Duarte, Ozan Varol, Eric Weiner, Lane Gardner, April Rinne, Mark Silverman, David Hayes, Jennifer Petter, Laura Gassner Otting, Michael O'Brien, Jeffrey Shaw, Paula Rizzo, Dave Melville, Kelly Wendorf, Amy Herman, Andrea Clough, Ann Brennan, Daniel Gutierrez, Paula Soteropoulos, Jeff Gothelf, Bob Coughlin, Franziska Iseli, Deirdre Breakenridge, Bill Harris, Tatiana Poliakova, Shelley Paxton, Alexis Artin, Amir Ghannad, Luke Timmerman, Steve Hoffman, Alice Pomponio, Jen Guillemin, Wendy Swart Grossman, Effie Park, Michael Hendrix, Panos Panay, Marshall Goldsmith, Ron Carucci, Alisa Cohn, Rob Walker, Nihar Chhaya, Larry Gennari, Hortense le Gentil, Ruth Gotian, Dan Norenberg, Alex Brueckmann, Tony Gambill, Joanne Kamens, Nancy Barrows, Hayden Lee, Alain Hunkins, Ramani Varanasi, David Taylor-Klaus, Diana Theodores, Darrin Tulley, Ed Evarts, Kristin Van Busum, Susan Finn, Bill Flynn, Tammy Gooler Loeb, Stacey Shipman, Nate Regier, Janice Litvin, Oleg Konovalov, Meredith Bell, Donna Loughlin, John Hagel, Mitchell Levy, Christof Zurn, Steven Morris, Amii Barnard-Bahn,

Michelle Johnston, Leslie Williams, Deb Coviello, Celine Schillinger, Michael Ku, Jeremy Utley, Chuck Wisner, Maryanne Spatola, John Baldoni, Jim Kerr, and so many more. If you are not listed, please know that you have also played an important role, and your omission is merely an oversight!

About the Author

**Tony Martignetti, Chief Inspiration Officer at Inspired Purpose Partners**, is a trusted advisor, leadership coach and facilitator, best-selling author, podcast host, and speaker. He brings together over 25 years of business and leadership experience and extreme curiosity to elevate leaders and equip them with the tools to navigate through change and unlock their true potential.

Before becoming the founder and Chief Inspiration Officer of Inspired Purpose Partners, he was a finance and strategy executive with experience working with some of the world's leading life sciences companies. Along his journey, he also managed small businesses and ran a financial consulting company.

He hosts The Virtual Campfire podcast and is the author of *Climbing the Right Mountain: Navigating the Journey to an Inspired Life* and the co-author of *Secrets of Next-Level Entrepreneurs*. He has been featured in many publications, including Fast Company, Forbes, Life Science Leader, and CEOToday.

Find out more about Tony at www.ipurposepartners.com, and check out the podcast at https://www.ipurposepartners.com/podcast.

Introduction

Why Are We Drawn to the Campfire?

Since the beginning of human history, stories have been told around fires to warn of danger, share wisdom, build trust, and inspire others. Stories hold power greater than we can imagine. They can ignite ideas and stir up feelings of awe, wonder, and inspiration. They can make us jump out of our seats in surprise or terror or warm our hearts. Sitting around a campfire and sharing stories is a timeless way of creating and feeling a sense of community. Yet, stories go beyond just books, movies, and theatrical performances. They also include the stories we tell ourselves about who we are as individuals and as a collective group. As a perpetual seeker of wisdom and community, campfires have always been a special place for me.

Before the COVID pandemic, I intended to start a group with like-minded people from every industry imaginable. I hoped to get inspiring people in a room together to share their journeys, wisdom, lessons, and struggles – a place of community and support. The original concept involved people sharing their stories in an intimate setting to provide ideas, feedback, and connection.

However, as that idea was taking shape and the keystones were being laid, the world shut down. Businesses were shuttered, and many of us were ordered to stay home. I had been working virtually for years by then, but I had hoped to build an in-person community, especially for people like me who thrive off being connected to a supportive community.

When the global pandemic derailed my plans, I decided to pivot and start a podcast instead. Although, initially, I was hesitant, could a podcast possibly provide the intimate experience I hoped to have? I could've never imagined the beauty that came with stepping out and trying something so far out of my comfort zone.

My name is Tony Martignetti, and for the past three years, I have hosted campfire conversations online through my podcast, *The Virtual Campfire*, where each episode features an inspiring guest who shares powerful lessons from their journeys through life.

DOI: 10.4324/9781003364818-1

My goal was to create a space for guests to feel safe to share the moments in their lives that ignited their gifts into the world through what I call "flashpoints." I wanted it to be a conversation that would take on a life of its own with no preconceived structure. What I uncovered were many stories and insights that were truly transformational.

It became clear that understanding our past experiences and behaviors can propel us forward into the future. But what does that mean? It means we must resist the urge to bury, deny, or minimize our past – even if it's painful. It means examining memories and experiences with a thoughtful and unbiased eye.

Ann Brennan, a *Virtual Campfire* guest, who had spent most of her life being "the strong friend and family member," came to a traumatic period when she was suicidal. Once she was past the crisis point, there was a lot of pressure to move on and pretend it never happened, to return to business as usual, blend in, and "be normal." However, Ann did the opposite. She embraced her story. She owned it, talked about it openly, and integrated it into her life.

Committing to owning our story can uncover things we never clearly understood about ourselves and others. The clarity we gain by understanding our past is a powerful gift. Embracing our past and integrating it into our present better position us to evolve to the next level of our human experience.

In Ann's case, she became an advocate for mental health, starting an organization that helps families struggling with depression and suicidal ideation. Though her life still has ups and downs, she has a strong sense of purpose and intention. Moreover, the connections she has made with other people feel stronger and more solid – after all, if you own your story, it becomes easier for the people around you to own and live theirs.

Truly understanding your past doesn't only benefit those who have faced life-or-death situations. For example, Ozan Varol, another *Campfire* guest, had spent years cultivating a visibly prestigious career, working on both the Mars Exploration Rover Project as well as graduating from law school and teaching law.

When he felt the calling to become an author who would help people reach their full potential, however, his head filled with opposing voices. What was he thinking, giving up a high-flying career with tenure? Who would he be without his "professor" title and all the other accolades he had earned? He's not alone – regardless of industry, personal circumstances, and demographics, people struggle with actively changing their future, even if they're not happy in their present.

The key for Ozan was to uncover his past. When he did, he realized that his achievement-focused successes in life had never made him happy. This realization gave him the courage to free himself from who he was (why hold on to what wasn't working for him?) and jump into who he was meant to be. He has since become a best-selling author (even though his book debuted at the height of the pandemic in 2020!) and a well-known blogger and podcaster.

When you see someone on stage sharing a powerful message, "owning the room," and having a huge impact in the world, you might ask yourself, how did they get that way? Were they born that way? Could I be like that person? What makes them different?

From the outside looking in, it seems like they are meant to do what they're doing. Many of us judge our insides by others' outsides. We see powerful people, and we think they may have some extra superpower or talent that we somehow lack. We wish we could embody their confidence, talents, or ability to achieve great things. The truth is, however, that we are all human. While some of us are born with natural gifts or interests, we all learn the lessons that life has to offer us one experience at a time, one moment at a time.

My goal was to share what you don't often see – their tales of transformation. The tiny steps that led to the big leaps. I wanted to bring people into a space where they share their stories because it inspires people. I get so lit up by the stories people share because it's meant to bring people to another place and to see that you made a lot of impact by sharing what you're doing in the world and how that can get others to take inspired action in their lives.

The Stories We Tell Ourselves

As I started interviewing people for *The Virtual Campfire*, I realized how powerful our personal stories can be. Our past is not something to run away from; it is something to embrace, reconcile with, and use as a powerful lever to move us into the future. When you commit to understanding and owning your true story, you uncover things you never clearly understood about yourself and others.

Sometimes the stories we tell ourselves don't serve us well. They keep us stuck and hold us back from realizing our full potential. When we allow our minds to focus on a limiting story such as "I'm not good enough" or "I will never be able to do this," it triggers the same cascade of stress hormones as if we were being chased by a tiger. We create our own nightmares through the stories we tell ourselves about what might happen. When we reflect on our past and rewrite our story, we can transform our past challenges into strengths.

Is it time to rewrite your story? If so, start by reconnecting with your past and reframing how you look at it. Here are a few questions for you to reflect on to begin to map out your story:

- What were the defining moments in my life or career?
- What were the flashpoints in my story that revealed my calling or gifts?
- What pain or challenge ultimately got me to step into action?
- What was the mindset shift I had to make to change my situation?
- What part of my past requires more closure or needs reconciliation?
- What are three lessons I have learned about myself?

I often talk about the concept of transcending and including your past when I work with clients. The philosopher Ken Wilber initially proposed this concept as a thinking principle that stated that "every new level of complexity transcends the earlier level's limitations and includes the less complex structure into itself." I like to think of it in simple terms: we have to embrace our past so we can integrate it and evolve to the next level of our human experience, our own personal evolution story. So how can you transcend and include your past?

My Journey from Corporate to Defining My Own Path

In my climb to the top, I gave up my health, my family time, my personal time, my time with friends, and in my darkest days, my desire to live, to serve a goal that was not ultimately mine. I shared my story so I could finally face my demons instead of running from them in the hope that I could move forward from a place of strength, not fear. I realized that my past could be a powerful lever for my future if I let it.

There came a day when I found myself sitting in yet another business meeting, looking around at a room of people who I knew were doing work that they had lost passion for and held no meaning to them. I knew because I had no passion for it either. I sat there, listening to a few executives argue about an insignificant issue. It was clear that they were fighting to save face and preserve their image. Meanwhile, I noticed how many people in the room were on their phones, totally checked out, and disinterested.

I had been working so long under the belief that "this is who I am, and this is what I do," but something inside me shifted that day. I realized I couldn't sit around and just collect a paycheck any longer. I'd been on this path too long where I had simply tolerated poor and, at times, toxic leadership.

The industry I was working in was founded on improving the health and well-being of so many people in the world, and I felt like we should no longer tolerate leaders that squander their opportunity to authentically lead, inspire, and empower the very people who make these amazing breakthroughs possible. So I decided at that moment that I couldn't do it any longer. I did something that I had never thought to do before. I left.

I stood up, walked out, and decided I wasn't coming back (at least not that version of me).

I realized that in order to change the room, I had to leave the room.

But how could I actually affect change? What should I be doing? If misguided leadership is the obstacle to a good workplace, where could I focus my energy to help remedy this problem?

The call came in the form of coaching. I wasn't sure how to become a coach, how my current skills would come into play, what new skills I would need to learn, or how I could make it into a business. Just like in my prior experience of being a very driven, ambitious overachiever, I dove into coaching head first. I got certified, learned as much as possible, and net-worked with gifted and experienced coaches, yet something was still missing.

I realized I had to do the work to understand myself more deeply. I had to go on an inner journey to discover who I was before I could guide others. I needed to fully see myself before I could be the person others could trust to guide them to create a better life for themselves and be a true explorer of human potential. Before I could help others go deep, I had to go deep myself.

I had to be transformed before I could transform.

According to Peter Bregman, "If you are willing to feel everything, you can have anything." When I read this quote for the first time, it felt like Peter gave me the words to describe the journey I had embarked on when I left the corporate world to become who I really am. I knew I had to have the emotional courage to explore deeper and answer the questions I was often afraid to answer.

As I think back to that day in the soul-crushing conference room, I made a choice that changed my life forever. A new me emerged with a fresh perspective. There were moments along the way, clues, and flashpoints, but this was the moment that truly shifted the momentum and created the necessary change in me. This moment called me to break the pattern that wasn't serving me and take the leap into a way of living that would be more aligned with my soul's purpose.

You see, I didn't know it at the time, but that was the beginning of my hero's journey. The very one Joseph Campbell distinguished in his famous writings. Like the classic stories, I had started in a world I knew, like the back of my hand. I then made a big choice and accepted the call to adventure. I traveled out into the unknown and experienced ups and downs, peaks, and valleys. I came across allies and foes, but eventually found the treasure.

The treasure was discovering myself, my way of making a difference, and my path to true fulfillment. Then I returned to the world I knew with knowledge and treasure to share with those also seeking it.

Why Uncovering the Past Resonates Now

The Great Resignation triggered by the pandemic has revealed both a changing relationship to work as well as a more significant social shift: people are tired of living lives where they feel stuck, where they feel their gifts aren't being put to use, where they spend most of their time just hanging in there or getting through the day. They're uncertain if they're on the right path and don't know what to do next. And they're looking for more than just platitudes or inspirational sayings on the side of a mug – they want practical, actionable advice that they can put to use.

This is where the power of storytelling and the campfire experience come into play. According to a study by the National Center for Biotechnology Information (NCBI), storytelling has been shown to increase empathy, understanding, and social connection. In fact, a 2018 study found that 65% of respondents felt more connected to others after sharing stories around a campfire. The same study also found that 80% of participants experienced reduced stress and increased relaxation when partaking in these gatherings. So it is not just me. Campfires are grounding experiences!

The American Psychological Association (APA) has highlighted the importance of narrative therapy, which uses storytelling to help individuals make sense of their experiences and find new meaning in their lives. This therapeutic approach has been shown to be effective in helping people find clarity, purpose, and personal growth.

As we grapple with the challenges of the Great Resignation and the post-pandemic world, the value of these campfire conversations becomes even more evident. By providing a platform for individuals to share their stories and the lessons they've learned, *The Virtual Campfire Podcast* is helping people understand their own journeys and find inspiration to make meaningful changes in their lives.

According to a survey conducted by Gallup in 2020, 64% of employees felt disconnected from their workplace, with many citing a lack of communication and shared purpose as contributing factors. By incorporating the principles of campfire storytelling into organizational settings, leaders can foster a sense of connection and belonging among their team members. This, in turn, can lead to increased engagement, collaboration, and overall job satisfaction.

Let's Get Grounded in How to Approach This Book

As I was thinking about bringing this book to life, I wanted to create a frame of mind to guide you, the reader, so that you could look for key themes along the way. As someone who works with leaders to challenge their mental models, I want to introduce something I have been thinking about lately. It is called grounded leadership, and it will be the perfect lens for reading this book.

So what is grounded leadership? First of all, I will start with leadership. Leadership is not just about how you show up in the workplace. It is about self-leadership and how you lead yourself inside and outside work. When you connect with this idea, you look at things from a different perspective and start making different life choices. So whether you are leading your team, company, family, organization, or group, it starts with leading yourself. However, this can be easier said than done. And as I continue to see, no one fully masters self-leadership; it requires continuous improvement as you move through life.

For you perfectionists out there, just because you can't win this game doesn't mean it is not worth playing. Effective self-leadership is the power-up you need to stay in the game and level up. Embracing self-leadership will unlock so many advantages in your life. You will be able to understand your unique strengths and how to leverage them effectively, have clarity of purpose, take more decisive action, and better connect with other people. It sounds like a worthy endeavor to me!

It starts by taking the journey inside to understand what drives your thoughts, feelings, and actions. This inner journey is why my coaching methodology is called Inside-Out Coaching because your inner transformation creates your outer transmission. The journey inside can unearth who you truly are through:

- Taking personal responsibility: discover what you can control and identify what actions or micro-steps you can take to move forward.
- Uncovering your beliefs: determine the code you live by. What are the "truths" you have chosen to believe about yourself, others, and the world?
- Revisiting your narrative: identify the stories you tell yourself about your past, present, and future.

As you take these steps, you become more self-aware, more emotionally courageous, and ultimately more connected to your unique way of leading yourself in the world. This leads to powerful self-leadership.

Once you have gained clarity from self-leadership, you can extend this new understanding to how you lead others, both directly and indirectly.

This is where the ripple effect comes into play! How you show up in the world and how you lead yourself and others ripple outward.

Now let's talk about being grounded. Being grounded generally refers to being fully present, balanced, and connected in your life. It involves a feeling of stability and inner peace, a deep connection with the earth and your surroundings, and a strong sense of self-awareness. Sounds great, right?

When we bring this together, it is something truly transformational. I think grounded leadership is the power to stay calm in the chaos. You remain centered and react without getting flustered or animated. Things come to you, and you respond with, "Ok, I can process this, and even if I don't have the answers, I can deal calmly with this situation." So you breathe it in, and you breathe it out.

What I like about grounded leadership is that this is based on the principles of nature. Nature's work gets done. It doesn't have to be managed. It knows when to let go and doesn't try to control anything. As the weather changes, it doesn't stress; it simply adapts.

This type of leadership is the path to lead us forward as individuals and collectively, and my goal is to create a mindset shift in as many people as possible around these ideas. The foundation of this new movement comes from taking intentional action grounded in three C's, which you will see throughout this book: curiosity, compassion, and connection.

So as you go on your journey through this book, I want you to keep the concept of grounded leadership and the three C's in mind and think about how they apply to how you lead yourself. Uncovering our past and dealing with trauma can propel us forward, and grounded leadership is a framework that can help you navigate the journey.

Before We Embark, A Personal Note

As I sit in front of my microphone, preparing to introduce yet another incredible guest to my podcast audience, I can't help but reflect on how this simple act of interviewing people has changed my life profoundly. What started as a way to connect humans has become a passion and a calling that has brought me so much joy and fulfillment.

Over the years, I have had the privilege of speaking with people from all walks of life – from successful entrepreneurs to world-renowned artists, from social activists to spiritual leaders. And what has struck me the most is the common thread that runs through their stories – the lessons they have learned, the challenges they have faced, and the wisdom they have gained.

Each guest has brought their unique perspective and experiences to the table, but certain themes have emerged time and time again. I have heard stories of resilience and determination, love and compassion, innovation, and creativity. And through it all, I have learned so much about what it takes to be a good leader, both personally and professionally.

One of the most powerful lessons I have gleaned from these interviews is the importance of mindfulness, of being present in the moment and fully engaged with the world around us. So often, we get caught up in our own thoughts and worries or distracted by the endless noise of the world. But when we can learn to quiet our minds and focus on what truly matters, we can unlock our full potential and lead more fulfilling lives.

This book will inspire and guide anyone who wants to become a better leader and cultivate a more mindful life. Through the stories and insights of these remarkable people, I hope to show that no matter where we come from or our circumstances, we all have the power to positively impact the world. So let's take a deep breath, listen (or read) deeply, and open our hearts to the lessons that await us.

End Notes

"Every new level of complexity transcends the earlier level's limitations and includes the less complex structure into itself." Wilber, Ken. *A Brief History of Everything.* Shambhala, 2000

"If you are willing to feel everything, you can have anything." Bregman, Peter. *Leading with Emotional Courage: How to Have Hard Conversations, Create Accountability, And Inspire Action On Your Most Important Work.* Wiley, 2018

Lesson 1

You Have the Power to Create Your World

Many people wish they could change their lives but feel powerless to do so. This feeling comes from believing their circumstances are unique and that a positive change is impossible for them. As we grow up, our environment and the people we depend on form our earliest beliefs about the world and our place in it. Some people hang onto these beliefs about what is possible their entire lives. The path is set, and they continue to follow what is there. However, some of the most successful people have pointed to one common lesson: we have the power to create our world.

To make this a reality, a mindset shift is required. It is essential to recognize that we are not defined by the stories we were born into; instead, we can alter our perspectives to align with our desires. While our circumstances at birth may be beyond our control, and life may present us with unforeseen challenges, our mindset remains within our control.

Let's dive into the concept of mindsets, focusing on both growth and fixed mindsets. Unfortunately, some individuals become trapped in a fixed mindset characterized by thoughts like "It is what it is" or "I can't help it." When Stanford University psychologist and author Carol Dweck published her revolutionary book, *Mindset: The New Psychology of Success*, she revealed a novel approach to examining how our beliefs and thoughts shape our experiences. Her extensive research distinguished between growth and fixed mindsets, highlighting that those with a growth mindset believe they can develop or change their traits over time, viewing the future as an opportunity for growth, even in challenging situations.

Examine your surroundings and consider what you wish they included. I frequently advise people I work with to channel their inner architect or interior designer for a moment. Assess your life as if it were a room with various elements. What can you rearrange, reimagine, repurpose, or redesign? What can you add or remove? How can you enhance its vibrancy and vitality? What steps can you take to create an environment more suited to your desired experiences?

DOI: 10.4324/9781003364818-2

Making a change doesn't require a grand project. It can begin with something as simple as repainting or altering the color scheme. You can implement small changes that eventually add up to a significant shift. For example, to improve your fitness, start with ten daily push-ups; to become more spiritual, meditate for ten minutes daily; and to expand your network, connect with three new people weekly and invite them for coffee or a conversation. Small actions should not be underestimated.

Feeling powerless often leads to persisting in one's current situation, hoping that hard work will eventually be rewarded. However, this approach is usually unsuccessful, draining you mentally, physically, and emotionally. Instead, by taking control of your situation and embracing your agency, you can create the life you desire, revealing a world of possibilities.

One of my favorite quotes is Picasso's "Every act of creation begins with an act of destruction." It resonates because dismantling old beliefs or thought patterns often precedes creating something new. We must unlearn to make space for new learning.

If you are wondering how you can create your own world, I recommend starting with my three C's of grounded leadership: curiosity, compassion, and connection. The first thing to get clear on is what you want. It is time to get curious! Step back from judgment for a minute and lean into what resonates with you deep down, at a soul level.

Begin by clarifying your vision and getting curious. What do you want your life to look like? Your vision doesn't have to be set in stone or something that pushes away other opportunities, but a general sense of what you want your life to look like. Ask yourself questions like: how do you want to feel? What do you want your days to be filled with? Where would you like to live? What would you like to do with your time? What are your priorities? Your vision is your true north, helping you navigate around or overcome obstacles in your pursuit, even if it entails lengthy detours.

Next, it's time to look at what's holding you back. Perhaps you are stuck in a fixed mindset? Try to apply self-compassion, especially when you recognize a belief that might paralyze you from taking action. These beliefs go back to our earliest lessons, but as we unpack them, we may realize that it is not the reality we are dealing with today. For example, if you are struggling with imposter syndrome, digging deeper into the root cause is helpful so you can learn ways to cope with it. Other obstacles can be more tangible or actionable. There may be a course you can take, a skill you need to learn, connections you need to make, or relationships to nurture. Whatever it is, write it down and explore ways to move forward.

Curiosity and compassion always lead me to connection. I love connecting with others on similar journeys so we can cheer each other on, share resources, and support one another. You don't have to embark on this journey alone; the more connections you establish, the more enjoyable and fulfilling the experience will be.

Remember that life doesn't have to change overnight, and you don't have to rush. Focusing on your desired feelings and priorities allows you to find the right direction, even if your true north evolves over time. Embrace the exploration process and take both small and bold steps toward your vision. Combining small actions with a few courageous leaps will lead to the right opportunities, enabling you to create your desired reality and ultimately transform your life.

Embracing an explorer mindset is the best way to embark on this journey. Being an explorer involves a lot of imperfect action. It is all about embracing novel ideas and perspectives. There are no expectations that you must be an expert when you are exploring. You just have to wonder what's around the horizon and pick things up and try them out. You ask questions of yourself and those around you. You collect information and learn what works and what doesn't. As an explorer, continuously learn and add to your knowledge base, recognizing that every experience counts. The journey and destination are equally significant.

With your explorer mindset in place, let me introduce you to some remarkable individuals who embody the spirit of exploration. Although their stories and journeys are distinct, they all exemplify the power of creating your own reality. They are all explorers in their own unique way and blazed unexpected trails.

Amir Ghannad: Turning Challenges into Opportunities

I met Amir Ghannad when I was invited to be a guest on his podcast, *The Transformative Leader Podcast*. We had an instant connection, having both worked at *Procter & Gamble* and shared a passion for transformative leadership. As I got to know Amir, I could see that he cared deeply about serving people and loved sharing the lessons from his past experiences with others.

Amir Ghannad is a highly sought-after keynote speaker at leadership summits in the United States and abroad. He is the co-founder and chief executive officer of The Ghannad Group, which offers speaking, workshop facilitation, and consulting services focused on guiding leaders in creating extraordinary cultures that deliver breakthrough results and unprecedented fulfillment.

For over 30 years, Amir held leadership positions of increasing responsibility and scope in multiple locations in the United States, Southeast Asia, and Europe. Amir's first book, *The Transformative Leader*, has been shipped to over 30 countries and is available in multiple languages. It's a fantastic book; having him on my show was an honor.

Amir moved to the United States from Iran during a tumultuous time in his home country. It was the late 1970s, and the Iranian Revolution had begun creating a period of civil unrest and harsh economic struggles. His parents sent him to America to get a high school education in Boston, with the expectation of him being able to return for visits and move back home when things settled down.

One of the things I ask all of my guests is to share with me their flashpoints, which are points in their lives that ignited their gifts into the world. This is what Amir shared about his first flashpoint that occurred shortly after arriving in the United States, *"Unfortunately, a couple of weeks after arriving, I got a fairly savage beating with broken bones. I tell you that part of my story because I lived a fairly sheltered life. I was the first grandchild in the family, and everybody loved me. Then I found myself in a situation where I had to fend for myself in a foreign country. My only means of communication with my parents was every two weeks, I would get a roll of quarters, go to a pay phone and get three minutes with them to let them know I was still alive."*

From a personal perspective, somewhere during those six months in Boston, it occurred to me that I have it in me to deal with whatever challenges come my way. Before that, I didn't relate to myself like that. Everybody always took care of me. I went from a shy kid with little confidence to someone who says, "If you're going to survive, you're going to have to fend for yourself."

When I think about having the power to create your world, I recognize that we can take all sorts of paths to reach that realization. However, we don't always realize the power of our choices when we make them; some become more evident when we look back at how those choices put us on a particular path.

For Amir, this moment was pivotal. Being alone in a foreign country with limited language skills and family support at such a young age sounds unimaginably challenging. Coming to America in the 70s was a different environment than today. The streets were tough, and Amir was not embraced as warmly as he might be today. I can only imagine the heightened discomfort that he had to deal with. The language barrier amplified his sense of loneliness, and indeed there were many things from a psychological perspective he had to contend with and overcome.

However, his perspective on what those hard times taught him is what is truly powerful:

"That loneliness, you open your eyes every day, and immediately realize, 'I don't know anybody.' It's a feeling of being homesick. What I would want to leave your audience with is that when we look back at those events and my experience, we could look at it and say, 'I don't even know how you made it.' The thing about it is we are far more resilient than we think.

So you do at the moment what you've got to do to get through the moment and not only survive, but grow to go on to thrive.

Nothing bad has ever happened to me, even though one might be able to point to a few things that would be labeled as 'bad' things. Every one of those things caused me to grow in some way. I feel blessed."

Instead of staying stuck in fear or despair, he began to see his experience as a gift that helped him grow on his journey. He went on to get a Bachelor's and a Master's degree in mechanical engineering from the Georgia Institute of Technology and an MBA from Wilmington University. Then he began his career in the corporate world of manufacturing leadership.

Amir's second flashpoint came several years into his professional career: *"I had a reasonably successful career. I had done some good things and was rewarded for it. But unfortunately, I found myself in a situation where I was managing a plant that wasn't doing well. The only thing worse than our results was our morale.*

I thought, 'I got this. I'm going to go in here to motivate and energize people.' However, it wasn't happening. I had to dig deep into what it is that I bring, how I can use my gifts and not just try to be this person or that person, but recognize what I can bring into this situation."

I can imagine that those folks thought, "Here comes another person who thinks he knows everything because he has a degree." What showed up for me at that point was that my superpower was not necessarily that I was a super engineer and I was going to come in and tell everybody what to do. "Instead, I discovered a superpower in empathy, listening, and getting into people's worlds."

Amir says his empathy and listening skills didn't necessarily push people to be their best. However, through much trial and error, he learned how to craft his leadership style to listen, commiserate, and then offer a path forward to encourage and motivate the people he worked with.

It's a reminder that we often don't come into our chosen career paths knowing everything and that part of having the power to create the lives we want involves our decision to act. In Amir's case, he recognized that to be a good leader required more than just continuing to refine the skills he already had acquired, but also being willing to stretch into new ways of thinking and relating to the world around him – and to himself.

Upon realizing the potential to make a real difference in people's lives, Amir and his wife founded The Ghannad Group, an innovative company that mentors leaders and individuals with comprehensive personal development solutions. Through their combined experience in manufacturing leadership, they empower others to cultivate positive change for themselves and society at large. On starting the company, he said, *"One of the things that we did was establish a two-part vision."* First, we said, *"We're going to be the showcase of excellence, which meant we were going to deliver the best results."*

"The second part was that we would be the cradle of prosperity, meaning we would enhance people's lives. This workplace is going to be a source of inspiration and prosperity."

Amir believes that every one of us contains the potential to be a transformative leader. Yet, life experiences can often prevent us from uncovering that potential and eat away at our ability to reach our full capacity. Only through self-reflection and openness toward growth can we unlock our inner leadership abilities, allowing ourselves to step into true transformation!

He says we have piled what he calls "the muckety-muck" on top of who we really are on the inside, which is magnificent. His book goes deeper into hidden saboteurs of success and fulfillment and how peeling the layers of the onion away can give you a glimpse of how powerful you are, how much good you can do, and how you can help others to tap into theirs.

"For me, the greatest lesson that I learned and what made a difference in that story that I told you about that turnaround was that I acknowledged it. At one point, it hit me that I was the culprit, the barrier to progress."

That was when I stopped asking, "Why is this happening to me?" Instead, I started asking, "Why am I tolerating this?" I created every problem I had, or I had at least contributed to it.

A cultural transformation has to start with personal transformation, looking at myself, getting to know me, not just my strengths and weaknesses, but how I handle situations. So that would be perhaps the most crucial lesson – start with yourself. I have this saying, "I am the one, and it's not about me." You must constantly remind yourself of this seemingly paradoxical idea of being the one, but it is not about you. "You have to take full responsibility and accountability as a leader."

Amir Ghannad's journey is a testament to the power of bravely creating your world. His story illustrates how individuals can rise above adversity, harness their innate abilities, and grow through self-reflection and personal transformation. By embracing his hardships and choosing to see them as opportunities for growth, Amir found his unique strengths and cultivated his empathetic, compassionate leadership style. His dedication to personal and professional growth is an inspiring example of how we all have the power to shape our lives and positively impact those around us. As we reflect on Amir's experiences, remember that our individual journeys, though filled with challenges, can ultimately lead to self-discovery, resilience, and transformation. By embracing our power to create our world, we can all strive to become transformative leaders, using our gifts to serve others and make a lasting difference in the world around us.

Dorie Clark: Embracing the Unexpected on a Journey to Discover Your Entrepreneurial Self

My conversation with Dorie Clark is one of my favorites to revisit for many reasons, primarily because she is warm, authentic, and witty. She has been a mentor and an inspiration to me long before our first conversation. She is someone who truly models the way for many thought leaders worldwide.

Dorie Clark has been named one of the Top 50 business thinkers in the world by Thinkers50 and has accumulated countless well-earned accolades and awards. However, it is hard to put Dorie into a category because she is engaged in so many things. She is a consultant and keynote speaker, teaches executive education at Duke University's Fuqua School of Business and Columbia Business School, and is the best-selling author of *The Long Game, Entrepreneurial You, Reinventing You,* and *Stand Out.*

At some point during my conversation with Dorie, I asked her if she had always wanted to be a journalist, and I was met with this wry reply, *"When I was a child, I wanted to be a spy because I loved James Bond. As I got older, I realized it would be a lonely job. You can't ever share your identity with others because you know how it is with spies, Tony. You've always got these people sleeping with you to get international secrets, and you can't trust anyone. You are having a great time. You meet a new friend and are suddenly being held at gunpoint. I thought, 'That's too stressful.' I realized that was ultimately not the right job for me. I am doing the next best thing now: writing a spy musical. That's my way of sublimating that desire."*

Dorie's story speaks to the power of staying open-minded to opportunities and delving into the power of networks. We began our conversation by talking about her early days as a journalist and the lessons she learned back then. She shared a story about being a young writer at a local newspaper and her experience with this one particular editor. Perhaps it was because she was the newest on the team, or maybe it was something more personal, but the editor didn't seem to be Dorie's biggest fan for whatever reason. Often, the editor would return her stories with red rivers of scathing feedback.

When Dorie submitted her first article to *The Boston Globe,* she talked about her personal satisfaction because they ran it as she had exactly as she'd written it, with no edits. It wasn't that she didn't understand that she had room to grow as a writer, but the knowledge that her talent was, in fact, the quality she knew it was, gave her that inner sense of knowing that her voice was powerful. However, she soon found herself forced into a career transition point.

"Flashpoint number one probably happened to me in my early twenties because I was a newspaper journalist. I thought I wanted to make a career as

a journalist. Instead, I got laid off and couldn't find another job. I didn't understand what was going on at the time. I thought it was a regular recession. Instead, as is sometimes the case in the world, it was a systemic disruption where the media industry was about to get its lunch eaten by the internet. As a result, no one was hiring, and I was forced to make a career change. Otherwise, I would still be a journalist. Instead, I went on a different path when I lost my job."

One thing that intrigues me about people is the story of their realization that they don't have to limit themselves to any one thing. You can be open to exploring your passions and the things you connect to as a child. For example, I was an artist when I was a child, and now, I find ways to connect with that as a coach and a guide for people to create their world.

I asked Dorie to describe what happened after her exit from journalism. What did her soul say to do next?

"My soul said had to find a job to pay my rent. That was the immediate thing. They gave me a week's severance pay. It wasn't even a week. It was four days because I had already worked Monday. What made it even more urgent was that I got laid off on Monday, September 10th, 2001. My first day of unemployment was not a good day to be looking for a job. Everything felt very urgent, and I needed to find work. I started freelancing, but as you can imagine, freelance journalism was not extraordinarily lucrative. I could scrape together a couple of articles a week, but that was $400, $600, or $800 a week if I had landed something good. I was scrambling to get revenue.

On the other hand, it was excellent training. When you study sports, they always say, "What you need is a concerted regular practice." The critical part that many people don't get is that you need immediate feedback, so you're not practicing the free throw with your elbow in the wrong place 900 times. You've got to have immediate feedback and correction to do it correctly.

The great thing about freelance writing is that that's what it is. You pitch ideas, and the editor says yes or no. So you get that feedback, and it's quick, decisive, and clear, and over time I had to become very good at quickly determining what was interesting as a news story and what was not. So I was able to hone my skills, which is still very valuable in the writing I do."

Being open-minded to feedback is a way of staying focused. The opportunities that arise when you're open to correction allow you to improve exponentially. Embracing constructive criticism can be a powerful way to drive your growth. By being open-minded, you create the potential for incredible leaps in both knowledge and progress. In Dorie's case, being open to opportunities to improve and grow led to her next career step.

"What brought me out of freelancing was a phone call in March of 2002 from a political consultant I frequently interviewed while writing for the

paper. He knew I had lost my job and reached out because he got hired by a candidate for governor. He was in charge of staffing the operation and asked if I'd be interested in applying as press secretary for this campaign.

This felt like a very fraught decision for me. Many years ago, a clear red line existed between being a journalist and working in politics. People go back and forth all the time now, but at the time, it was a big deal that if you were a journalist and you crossed over, you were closing the door. You were not allowed to be a journalist anymore. That was the conventional wisdom at the time, or at least how people in the journalism industry thought about it. Now it's different, but back in the day, it was very sacrosanct. Some old-school reporters wouldn't even vote because they like to be perfectly impartial.

It was very stressful. Did I feel ready to give up this dream that I've been harboring? This was an opportunity. It was so clear that there were two doors that I could walk through. So I should err on the side of saying yes."

With that willingness to embrace an opportunity gained through networking to step into a new career, she accepted the interview, was hired, and began her career in politics.

After that campaign job ended, she realized her next big goal was to work on a presidential campaign. So, once again, Dorie leaned into her network to see what opportunities were available. She goes deeper into the process in her books, but what stood out to me was that boldly leaning into her network and being open to the results ultimately landed her the job she was looking for. Since she wasn't married to a particular ideology, party, or person, she could cast a wide net to see what path opened up.

She shares the power of mutually beneficial relationships in networking and how connecting the right people in the right places is less about meritocracy and more about finding the right fit.

"I think it's similar to the age-old thing of the jocks in high school who don't appear to work hard, and all they do is play football. So how is it that they're able to be so popular, successful, and get good jobs? They didn't do the work. They didn't get straight A's. It's not fair.

We must realize that life is not run on the same metrics as school is. Our parents are doing us a disservice, and we are doing ourselves a disservice to cling to this idea that meritocracy means that you excel on a certain narrow set of parameters that determine your worth. That's ridiculous. It's good to be good at school, but that's not the only thing.

Life is a lot bigger and broader than that. It's unfair if someone lazy, untalented, and unqualified gets placed somewhere, which sometimes happens. However, much more often, someone who is adequate can ascend to the top because, in addition to being sufficient at whatever the metric is, they are great at some other metric that perhaps we haven't considered.

Ultimately, it's much more helpful to look at other people with success or things we want and try to reverse engineer it and say, 'What exactly did they do? How exactly did they do it?' Then, assuming they didn't break some law or something shady, we need to start thinking, 'How can I do more of that? How can I emulate that rather than criticize it?'"

When she shared that, it made me think of the classic quote, "Success is where preparation meets opportunity," but expanding on it further by acknowledging the importance of adding the element of a powerful network to the mix. Success is where preparation, networks, and opportunities meet!

Dorie had acquired the skills needed to do the job, had the right people helping get her resume on the right desks and recommending her personally, and was open to the opportunities that showed up rather than limiting her options with narrow thinking.

After the campaign ended with the candidate she worked for not being elected, she returned to Boston to run a bicycling advocacy nonprofit. She decided to go out and start her own business. She would have never thought about running her own business had she not had the experiences that led her to that decision.

"It was not a desire I had harbored for a long time. It would not have occurred to me were it not for all the steps along the way. Running this little tiny bicycling nonprofit was this bizarre career aberration because I wasn't even a good bicyclist. I was a terrible bicyclist, but it was great because, running this small organization, you have to do everything. You have to adopt the mindset of an entrepreneur where if you're not going to do it, it isn't getting done. You have to roll up your sleeves and figure it out, even if you don't want to."

That is the kind of mindset that is very helpful for entrepreneurs. You know you are responsible for everything and have to make it get done even if you don't know how.

A problem I see in many coaching clients or people I come across is this golden handcuff situation where people may have worked in the corporate world for a long time. They would like to go out on their own, but they have gotten used to a lucrative corporate salary and feel it's risky. It's tough if you're making a lot of money already. It's hard to replicate that instantly. We all kind of know this intuitively. It takes some time to build up.

My situation was I was not making a lot of money at all. So I looked at being an entrepreneur and said, "Literally, almost no matter what I do, I can make more money than this."

When asked what advice she would give to others, whether just starting on their journeys or who find themselves at a pivot point of their own, she shares:

"From the time we're young, a lot of people are very willing to cede authority to other people and to say, 'If this authority figure says that they don't like it, this isn't good enough, or this isn't right then I guess they're

correct and I'm wrong. They're correct, and I'm not good enough.' I cannot emphasize enough that God did not anoint these people.

They likely have no idea what they're doing, and we should not trust implicitly that their judgment is better than ours. You don't want to be mulish about it. If 100 people tell you that it's not right, you can probably trust their judgment. If one person tells you, they could be having a bad day. They could be a person with bad judgment. Who knows?"

Dorie is an accidental entrepreneur, but there is no doubt she has been successful. When you reflect on the formula of success, she prepared herself at every turn to use what she learned to move forward to her next step while being committed to the long game. She also provides a great example of how to build connections effectively and leverage them to open up new opportunities.

Dorie Clark's journey is a testament to creating your own reality. Her ability to remain open-minded and adaptable to new opportunities, combined with her innate talent and perseverance, allowed her to forge a unique path to success. Dorie's story serves as a potent reminder that we all can shape our destinies by embracing our passions, honing our skills, and leveraging the power of our networks. By staying true to ourselves and being open to change, we can create the world we envision, one step at a time. So, whether you're at the beginning of your journey or facing a pivotal moment, remember that you have the power within you to create a world that aligns with your dreams and aspirations.

Effie Park: Building Communities through Self-Discovery and Advocacy

Effie Park's story immediately popped into my head when I thought about people having the power to create their own world. I see her as someone who found herself thrust into a world she never expected and then blazed a trail to create her own place to fit in, and in the process, built a community and a safe place for others in similar situations.

Effie hosts the *Once Upon a Gene Podcast*, where she speaks to her guests about their journey through life with a rare disease. Since the podcast's launch, the show has won numerous awards, and Podcast Magazine recognized Effie as one of the 40 Under 40 Podcasters. She describes her mission as lifting the voices of the community, connecting people with resources, and leaving the world better than she found it for others in the rare disease world.

In life, we may not know where we fit or what to do next, but there is an opportunity for transformation. We can utilize difficult situations that bring up feelings like discomfort, fear, and isolation and transform them to reach the depths of our capacity that we didn't know we had.

Such is the case with Effie, who found herself with a newborn son who seemed uncomfortable in his body from day one. Effie shares the story of a baby who didn't eat well, cried inconsolably, and struggled for the first few months of his life.

"When my son, Ford, was born, we were so excited. We had all of these ideas of what it would be like to have a child, and what they would be like. We had all these things planned out for this fictional person. As soon as we brought him home, we started having a lot of difficulties feeding him. I couldn't get him to breastfeed. We couldn't get a bottle down him.

It would take three hours sometimes to get a couple of ounces down him. Most of the time, the milk would be on his chest or coming out the sides of his mouth. He cried all the time. We kept telling our pediatrician that something wasn't right. Ford wasn't eating. He was writhing in pain. We got brushed off a lot as new parents and were told that 'every baby cries, every baby stays awake, They're just colicky, that's it. Try this, try that, go home.' We kept going in.

We were both on maternity and paternity leave, so we had all the time to keep banging on doors. Once a week, we saw pediatricians. We were seeing lactation specialists. We weren't taking no for an answer, even though we were constantly told everything was fine.

After three months, our pediatrician turned to us in our appointment. She looked horrified and said, 'Effie, I've made an appointment for Ford at Children's Hospital. I'm worried about him.'

I remember that moment vividly. I remember finally feeling validated that she listened. But I also remember being so angry at her and so betrayed by her.

My son was immediately admitted to the hospital. The doctor looked at me and said, 'Ford has microcephaly. He has hypotonia.' She rattles off these things. Finally, I realized that she thought I knew. She thought my doctor had told me what her concerns were with Ford. I had never thought about anything serious. I just knew something was wrong. Did I believe that these things had an actual name or a diagnosis? Not in a million years. He looked like everybody else's baby. He didn't look like there was something wrong with him. Hearing all this stuff was a shock. Those were traumatizing experiences.

I don't remember a lot of the aftermath of those moments. Somehow, they have evaporated. They are buried, maybe in the trauma of those moments of getting this information about my child. When we were let home, they had set up things with early intervention programs. That got the ball rolling to determine what was wrong with my son.

I feel lucky that this happened the way it happened because I know families like mine sometimes don't get these answers for years. They don't push for answers and get told the answers. It can be a complex world to navigate. It still is, but luckily a geneticist took some interest in my son because he's exceptionally white. He lacks pigment in his skin, has white hair, and has eye issues from transillumination. His skin is so white that she thought it was a fatal type of albinism.

She was intrigued and helped push for the tests to get that answer, which, thank goodness, because I don't know if I would have a diagnosis for Ford if something hadn't piqued her interest, like a unique diagnosis of albinism."

Effie describes having a moment of realization once the shock wore off, where she looked back over Ford's earliest days and was frustrated that she had not pushed harder for answers or simply switched doctors. It opened up her eyes. As she said, *"I didn't know I could necessarily forge my own path until it happened."*

This led Effie to the news she didn't expect, which would change her life's trajectory forever. *"The geneticist called us and told us Ford had a diagnosis, but it wasn't what she expected. She said it was CTNNB1. She read two papers on it. Some kids could say a few words and take several steps. He was 1 in 30 in the world, period, end of the meeting. We were not offered resources and hope; we were limited and isolated. Luckily, I found a Facebook group. She had underestimated the prevalence of the disease; there were over 50 people in the group. I finally felt like there were other parents like me. There was not much to look towards since the kids' ages were all young. I didn't necessarily have an older kid to get insight from, but it felt so good to have someone who knew this foreign word, this gene. I felt comforted by that.*

I discovered this world of Facebook groups. I didn't know that was a thing. I found groups for parents who had kids with feeding tubes. I saw groups for parents who had kids with microcephaly, all of the symptoms that my son had due to CTNNB1. It started to open some doors for me because, aside from this, I was so alone and isolated. All my friends with kids the same age, and the gap between the development was miles now. They were going to the park, and I was holding my son down to put the feeding tube back down his nose because he vomited it up. I couldn't relate to them, and they couldn't relate to the loneliness and fear that grew in me.

The longer it continued, the more aware I was that this stress, this isolation, this achiness was manifesting in my body because I hadn't necessarily let all of it move through me. I was in the car for at least four hours a day, getting Ford to and from appointments for a couple of years.

He had appointments five days a week. I would listen to podcasts and stories. I found a few on the topic of what I wanted to hear, of other families like me or anyone talking about this lifestyle. When I discovered podcasts, everything changed for me. It was the first time I felt like someone understood what I was going through. I didn't have a relationship with these people, but I related to them, and they helped me.

There weren't a lot of podcasts in this world a few years ago. There were less than ten that I could find that didn't quit, had more than three episodes, and weren't garbage.

When that content dried up, I couldn't have it. That was not an option for me because it opened my eyes to the fact that there is a community. I need to find them. I remember walking outside with my son. I always walked with him for hours and would have my headphones on. I knew that I needed to do this. I could do this. I have listened to enough podcasts to know I can do this.

I knew that it was a piece of my purpose, and it was so loud. I don't know what it was. It was something that called to me, and I just did it. I started a podcast for not only myself. I wanted to be that person on the other end, like that parent in the car weeping could find and feel a little less alone."

This is a flashpoint moment like none other. First, it was identifying that there is a missing piece in the world that would impact people's lives in such a big way and then realizing that she could be the one to do it. Effie has done a fantastic job building that podcast into a beautiful platform. She brings people's stories to life.

She saw a need to help people feel less alone and created a platform for people to share not just what's on their minds but in their hearts. I find so much beauty in this. So many people suffer alone, and the trials and tribulations of being a parent of a child or even being a patient who suffers from one of these rare diseases. Effie is championing these people and creating a world where they can connect.

Effie shared that she's always listened to others and held space for their stories. She's worked as a hairstylist, a waitress, a bartender, and a telemarketer – all careers where listening is an active part of what makes someone successful.

"I've heard people's stories for as long as I can remember. People like talking to me. I like listening to people because I can find things in other people's journeys that resonate with me. I can see the parts that are important to them, especially hearing someone's voice. I feel like there's so much power in that and how much it can resonate with you over this magical medium of podcasting when you can hear their soul."

Years of going through her own journey revealed this hidden gift of being able to be empathetic with what people are dealing with. *"I feel like we could all hone our listening skills a little more – giving people the permission to do or feel however they need to feel. What they need is space."*

I asked her what the most powerful lessons she learned about herself and about her journey to self-advocacy that she wanted to share with people, and this is what she had to say: *"I have learned so many lessons about myself. One of the big ones that shifted my mindset was knowing that I didn't have to handle it and carry it, be strong, be responsible, and use all the coping skills I have to manage it. I could just know that it sucked. I could have bad days and not be a bad mom or feel sorry for myself, but be aware of all the terrible stuff happening and accept it.*

There's nothing wrong with those feelings. I was so jealous of your kid when I watched them blow out their birthday cake. I'm not ashamed that I'm jealous of that. I am. It's part of it. It's one of my emotions.

It was big for me to realize that I could accept those for what they are and not feel ashamed of them. It helped my throat. It helped me breathe again when I was okay with going through the motions and the emotions.

It's much more enjoyable when you put yourself in that mindset to watch even how much more skilled you can become at allowing these emotions to be there and then flit away. You build some muscle memory for it in some way."

Effie Park's journey demonstrates the power each of us holds to create our own world, even amidst challenging circumstances. Faced with an unexpected reality and feeling isolated, Effie recognized a need to connect people within the rare disease community. By embracing her own strengths and experiences, she forged her path and created the *Once Upon a Gene Podcast.*

Through her dedication, Effie not only transformed her own life, but also built a supportive community that fosters connection, understanding, and hope for others facing similar challenges. Her story is a powerful reminder that while life may not always go as planned, we can choose how we react to it and find strength in our resilience. By embracing our ability to create our own world, we can also create spaces that empower and support others. So, as we navigate life's inevitable challenges, let us remember the power we possess to shape our experiences and create a more inclusive and understanding world for all.

The Lessons

We might not have much control over what happens in the world around us, like the weather, the economy, or how people behave, but the one thing we do have control over is our own actions and the choices we make every day. Sure, we won't always make perfect decisions or have all the answers, but the important thing is that we get to decide how we handle life's ups and downs. By focusing on what we can control, we can learn from our experiences, grow as individuals, and ultimately shape our own paths, no matter what life throws at us.

Amir Ghannad's journey demonstrates the power of creating our world in the face of adversity. Through his experiences, we learn the importance of self-reflection, personal transformation, and embracing challenges as opportunities for growth. By harnessing our innate abilities and staying open to change, we can unlock our true potential as leaders and positively impact the lives of those around us. Amir's story is a powerful reminder that we all possess the strength and resilience to rise above difficulties and create a meaningful, fulfilling life. By recognizing and embracing our power to create our world, we can become transformative leaders who serve others and make a lasting difference in the world around us.

Dorie Clark reminds us of the importance of being open-minded, adaptable, and leveraging the power of networks in creating our own world. Dorie's journey from journalist to best-selling author and business thinker demonstrates the significance of embracing change, pursuing passions, and continuously honing our skills. By staying true to ourselves and being receptive to new opportunities, we can shape our destinies and forge our unique paths to success. This powerful lesson reminds us that we can create a world that aligns with our dreams and aspirations, whether we are just starting our journey or facing a pivotal moment in our lives.

Effie Park's journey demonstrates the power each of us holds to create our own world, even amidst challenging circumstances. Faced with an unexpected reality and feeling isolated, Effie recognized a need to connect people within the rare disease community. By embracing her own strengths and experiences, she forged her path and created the *Once Upon a Gene Podcast*. Through her dedication, Effie not only transformed her own life but also built a supportive community that fosters connection, understanding, and hope for others facing similar challenges. Her story is a powerful reminder that while life may not always go as planned, we can choose how we react to it and find strength in our resilience. By embracing our ability to create our own world, we can also create spaces that empower and support others. So, as we navigate life's inevitable challenges, let us remember the power we possess to shape our experiences and create a more inclusive and understanding world for all.

Questions

As we wrap up this lesson, let's circle back to the three C's of grounded leadership: curiosity, compassion, and connection, with some questions for you to ponder and journal.

- Think of a time you've been brave. What did that feel like? What actions were you able to take? What was the result?
- When have you pushed back against someone trying to discourage you? Or what tried to derail you that you were able to stay the course with? What actions did you take, and how were you able to stand up for yourself?
- What opportunities are open to you now? What have you always been interested in exploring, but haven't yet? Who are the people you could reach out to help you on your journey?

- Have you searched for a place to connect with others? If you haven't found the right group, what would it look like to create it? Who would you want to support and be supported by?

End Notes

"Every act of creation begins with an act of destruction." (Picasso)
Mindset: The New Psychology of Success – Carol Dweck
The Transformative Leader – Amir Ghannad
Stand Out – Dorie Clark
Entrepreneurial You – Dorie Clark
Reinventing You – Dorie Clark
The Long Game – Dorie Clark

Out of Darkness Comes the Light

Often, our darkest days become the source of our greatest strengths, although it doesn't feel like it at that moment. We must go through life's crucibles to find true meaning and purpose. Through the stories of many inspirational people who have navigated their darkest moments, we can see that hope is the most powerful thing we have to navigate traumatic times. When we hold onto hope and use the knowledge we learn during challenging times, we can find ways to harness experiences into powerful shifts in our lives. These shifts can create a positive impact on ourselves and many others. This lesson will share how to find the hope you are looking for and leverage it to uncover the light inside the darkness so you can create a powerful future.

No one is immune to the pain and grief, especially when we are going through our darkest times. However, we all differ in how we navigate grief and what we take from it. For many, suffering may become all-consuming; for others, it can push us outside our comfort zone to find growth or a new life purpose.

Let's explore the emotional experience of grief for a moment. Grief is not just one emotion. It is a spectrum of emotions that might include sadness, anger, guilt, confusion, anxiety, and many others. So, what are emotions, and what do they represent? Emotions are signals. In the book *Emotional Intelligence 2.0*, Travis Bradberry and Jean Greaves explain that emotions are neither good nor bad. They are simply indicators from within that tell you something is happening in your environment. It's no secret that emotions can significantly impact your life, and how you manage them can disrupt your life, either negatively or positively.

The impact of grief or trauma and the associated emotions can sometimes lead to post-traumatic growth, a theory developed by psychologists Richard Tedeschi, Ph.D., and Lawrence Calhoun, Ph.D., in the mid-90s. As Tedeschi explains, "People develop new understandings of themselves, the world they live in, how to relate to other people, the kind of future they might have, and a better understanding of how to live life." This growth

DOI: 10.4324/9781003364818-3

leads them to shift their mindset and how they experience and manage their emotions.

To become a dynamic leader, you must learn to navigate the darkness and the light, meaning we must be more intentional about understanding our emotions. Facing our feelings head-on, getting curious about them, and practicing emotional intelligence can be game-changing. Our emotions are often deeply rooted and seem beyond our control, but we can better manage our emotions with awareness and by developing effective coping strategies. Cultivating this emotional agility will enhance your leadership skills and foster healthier relationships and personal growth.

Many of us have barometers of our own emotional health. For example, when going through tough times, we may notice that our behavior in traffic could be better. Or we may be short with family members when we are stressed out. We might even see our internal monologue getting more abrasive and harsh. However this shows up for you, take notice of this signal as a guide to your emotional health.

Leaders should consider applying the three C's of grounded leadership: curiosity, compassion, and connection as the foundational components of the human emotional management system and bringing each one to the table as they explore their moments in the darkness and how they can come into the light.

Quite often, we live our lives on autopilot and react to strong emotions without truly understanding what they mean. But think of feelings as an inner compass — a signal that helps guide you through all facets of life. So when you face something challenging, take the time for self-reflection by asking yourself: "What is this feeling trying to tell me?" Taking ownership and gaining that insight can be a powerful tool for making decisions that lead in the right direction.

Connection is a remarkably effective tool for navigating challenging times. When we're going through a difficult time, it's easy to feel isolated and alone. However, it's important to remember that we are not the only ones who have gone through tough times, and people are willing to help us if we can ask for it. But it's not just about receiving help – it's also about giving back. By focusing on connection and service to others, we can find meaning and purpose in our lives and gain a perspective that can help us escape our darkness. So feel free to seek help when needed, and remember to lose yourself in service to others.

I'd like to share an easy exercise for beginning the process of digging deeper into your emotional well-being and learning how to use them as an asset, even in the darkest of times.

The first step to effectively managing your emotions is to acknowledge them. Acknowledging feelings is difficult for many people and emotional habits are often embedded in us from an early age. Looking back at the people you were surrounded by growing up, how they managed emotions during difficult times subconsciously impacted us. If someone you considered a role model bottled up their feelings and blew up later, you may emulate that behavior. Or if your role model withdrew when they struggled with emotions, you might do the same. Whatever the case, our emotional management system begins early in our development.

We can change the narrative when we become conscious of how we manage our emotions. Next time you experience a strong emotion about a challenging situation, take a moment and acknowledge how you feel. Then, see if you can describe it or name it. Once you have the name in your sights, you can manage it from a conscious perspective instead of an emotional one.

Next, it's time to let your feelings flow. Once you've given the way you are feeling a name, recognize that the emotion you are feeling is there for a reason; it is trying to tell you something; it has a purpose to serve. When you take the time to do this, you will connect deeper within yourself and determine what the feeling you are experiencing truly means. It may take some time, but eventually, it will make sense. If you are stuck on this one, writing down your thoughts in a journal can be helpful. Put pen to paper and just let the words flow. There is no pressure for journaling to be perfect or even make sense. Just write your thoughts down and explore them to determine what your body and mind want you to learn.

Third, shift your focus to understanding. Once you've had a chance to process how you are feeling, it's time to ask yourself what the lesson or the gift attached to the feeling is. Keep in mind that not all lessons initially feel positive; it is only through time and reflection that we can fully understand them. Sometimes this third step can be the most difficult to process. If you feel a little stuck, turn to your journal and jot down your thoughts. Think of a time when you felt like you are now. What did you learn, and how does it relate to what you are feeling now?

Finally, use what you have learned to decide what you want to do next. Each experience contributes to who we are meant to be, so each lesson learned is a step in our journey to becoming ourselves. But knowledge alone is not enough; what you do with this new awareness makes all the difference.

Using the four steps above, you can be on the path to understanding your emotions and utilizing the lessons learned to grow personally and professionally.

In this chapter, we will explore the stories of a few incredible individuals who encountered their darkest moments and reframed them as the foundation to create healthy, fulfilling, and empowering lives. Through their stories, we can see how they found hope, strength, and resilience during the most challenging periods of their lives. Their experiences demonstrate that embracing the three C's of grounded leadership – curiosity, compassion, and connection – can guide us through our darkest days and empower us to emerge stronger, more compassionate, and more connected to ourselves and others.

As you continue reading, remember that your own journey will be unique, but the principles we explore together can be universally applied. Be open to learning from the experiences of others and be prepared to adapt their insights to your personal growth and leadership development. With time, practice, and intention, you can use the power of hope and the lessons learned during difficult times to create a meaningful and impactful life.

Ann Brennan: The Power of Sharing Your Story

I met Ann Brennan as a guest on her podcast, *ASMM Small Business Connections Podcast*, where we discussed managing stress and avoiding burnout. Her passion for supporting small businesses was incredible, and her upbeat attitude was contagious. I couldn't wait to spend more time with her.

Ann is the CEO of ASMM Digital Marketing, a digital agency that helps small businesses create a community around their brand, building engagement through services including social media, website management, content creation, graphic design, and other forms of digital marketing. Ann is also the founder of Burgers and Bands for Suicide Prevention, a non-profit organization and community event created alongside her son Ethan dedicated to raising money and awareness for mental health and suicide prevention. Ann sees ending suicide as her life purpose and is passionate about encouraging companies to embrace cause marketing.

Ann, aka Iron Ann, was everyone's strong friend – the one no one thought they needed to worry about. And when I met Ann, it was clear why she was labeled "the strong friend." In October 2012, Ann had just finished the iconic Ironman race, but little did she know an even more significant challenge was just around the corner.

Outside of being Iron Ann, she was also a mom to two boys. Shortly after completing her Ironman, Ann noticed something wasn't quite right with her son, Ethan, and only a few short months later, Ann found herself with a son who was self-harming, suicidal, and hospitalized. As a parent, we have expectations of being able to keep our children safe and healthy, so imagine the shock to the system when, despite doing everything in your power, you have a child who is struggling.

By July 2013, Ann's own mental health had rapidly declined, and she felt utterly hopeless about Ethan's challenges. She could no longer see the light at the end of the tunnel. She began planning how to cope with life if her teen son died. Her racing thoughts about Ethan's continued struggles and neglecting her own basic needs, including proper nutrition and rest, created a dangerous situation for Ann.

It is often those we least expect that suffer in silence, isn't it?

She recalls driving one day and thinking she should just head over to the bay bridge and jump off. This thought stopped her in her tracks, and it was at this moment she realized that she, the strong friend, desperately needed help. She immediately called a local psychiatric facility and explained how she was feeling.

"It's a dark moment of no hope. People say, 'I don't understand why somebody would die by suicide.' They have lost all hope. For me, I lost all hope. In my mind, Ethan was going to die, which meant my life had to end because I could not live without him. That was where I was, whether it made sense or not, whether this was where we were or not, it's where I was."

Little did Ann know at the time, that call would be the one that changed her life. After a week-long stay in the facility, something shifted in Ann, and she knew she needed to use her story to show others that sometimes you yourself are the strong friend that needs to be checked on.

Upon discharge, Ann wrote a blog post to share her story and immediately received a comment from someone that he had reached out for help before taking his own life. Once seeing the impact sharing her story had, it confirmed what Ann knew – our stories matter. By being vulnerable with who we are and what is real for us, we can create genuine connections – the reward for overcoming our shame or isolation. Sharing her story kickstarted the development of Burgers and Bands Suicide Prevention.

Ann recounts, *"I help people get their message out there, and that's a powerful thing to do. I look back on that day and think, 'What if I hadn't called for help?' And now, it's powerful to look back and say, 'I have done all these things. I'm impacting somebody's life.' Every day, we get to impact somebody's life, whether we know it or not.*

I wrote a blog post called Psych Ward Annie. My husband was furious with me. He was like, 'I cannot believe you did this. Why would you put yourself out there this way? This is our private information.' We had been married for several years and never argued, even with everything we went through with Ethan. We were always there for each other, but he was so mad at me at this moment.

At the time, I told him, 'People are calling me Iron Ann, and I spent a week trying to pull myself back up because I wanted to die. I can't do that. It's not fair to people to think of me as this strong person when that's what almost killed me. It's being a strong person, not admitting that I was having a hard time, not telling people that I don't know how to deal with these emotions that I'm having for my child, this fear that I'm dealing with.'

We were arguing. I had my phone in my hand, and it buzzed at me. I looked down, and there was a comment from my blog, it was from a fifteen-year-old boy, and he said, 'I was going to kill myself tonight, but I called my mom, and she's going to come to help me.' At that moment, my husband said, 'What else can we do? How else do we share this?' Everything changed for us."

I felt emotional hearing Ann share this part of her story. Her courage in sharing her story literally saved someone's life. That moment was pivotal. For Ann, it was the reflection she needed to hear in order to shake off the shame and see herself and others who ask for help as courageous.

"There's so much shame around it. For the longest time, I felt ashamed that I had let myself get to this place. When I was in the hospital, my husband visited and asked 'What happened?' I said, 'I told you I was struggling.' He said, 'You said, "I'm struggling," but you didn't say you were suicidal. There's a big difference between these two.'

That moment of that young man saying, 'I'm going to get help,' took a lot of that shame away because I could see how strong he was. That was strong for him to tell his mom, which meant if it was strong for him, I had to be strong as well. So it was an eye-opener for me and our entire family."

Realizing the strength it takes to ask for help and the power of being vulnerable, Ann became determined to create a path for others to do the same.

For years, Ann and her family participated in fundraising walks for suicide prevention but felt called to have a more significant impact. So they started an event-based organization called Burgers and Bands for Suicide Prevention, which has raised thousands of dollars and brought mental health programs into several schools and organizations. Their tagline, "You Are Not Alone," strives to help alleviate the loneliness of those who suffer from depression and suicidal ideations. Their goal is to get the word out to people in the community that they are not alone and that help and hope are available.

Outside of the charity, Ann runs a digital marketing company and has a podcast. In our conversation, I realized that her many roles all focus on helping people tell their stories, much like she did back when she needed to be heard the most. Sometimes, the beauty of reflecting on our past is that we see the underlying themes we don't usually notice.

"I look back on that day and think, 'What if I hadn't called for help?'

I think of all of the people I have been able to help, businesses I have helped grow, or entrepreneurs I have gotten in front of people who have said they can share their message to a charity we started. What would have happened to all these things I have done if I hadn't called for help? And above all else, my children, what would have happened to them? It's powerful to look back and say, 'I have done all these things in this short time. Every day, I'm affecting somebody's life.' Every day we all affect somebody's life, whether we know it or not."

One story that Ann shared almost knocked me out of my chair because it reinforced the power of sharing honestly and that you may be surprised how much the person right next to you can relate:

"This one particular night, I received a text message from a woman. She said, 'I am struggling. I need help.' I asked if she needed help immediately or if she'd like help finding a therapist. She said, 'I need a therapist. I'm not suicidal. I'm okay, but I'm struggling with some dark thoughts.' So I said, 'Okay.'

I'm texting her, and at the same time, I get a text from another woman. She said she needed help. When I asked if she was suicidal, and she said yes, I asked permission to call 911 and she agreed. When I asked her if there was anyone that she could call to be with her while I called the ambulance, she said, 'There's nobody I can share this with.' Meanwhile, I'm still talking to the woman in the other text, and I asked if there was anyone she could talk to, she said 'There's nobody.'

I swear, it sounds like I made the story up; these two women actually run together every morning. They had never told the other one they were struggling. To me, it shows you don't know. Now they are huge advocates of what we do, and they share their stories out loud. It's so important that we do that because if one of them had turned to the other, they may not have gotten to where they would be in that dark place."

The tagline for my business is "Inspiration through honest conversation." I think about all the things people don't have conversations about and the things they don't bring to the surface. Honest conversations not only inspire us, but they also connect us at a deeper level. Humans are wired for deeper connection; it bonds us, inspires us to take action, and helps us feel a sense of belonging instead of being alone and isolated.

Ann Brennan's story of her struggle with darkness has raised money and helped countless people, including her family. She shared about the many people that come to her with stories of their own darkness, whether that be loss, drug addiction, abuse, or mental health issues. Ann found strength in vulnerability and discovered the power of sharing her story. As we reflect on Ann's story, we are reminded that when we are brave enough to share our darkest moments, we can emerge from the shadows and bring light to both ourselves and others. Ultimately, it is through honest conversation, the courage to ask for help, and the power of connection that we can truly illuminate the lives of those around us.

Lane Gardner: Finding Your Creative Voice to Heal Trauma

Everyone has trauma that needs to be healed. One way of healing is by using the power of art. It can be anything from writing to acting. You just need to find what medium fits you to start your healing process. For Lane Gardner, music was her medium, so she became a songwriter, using her music to heal people's trauma.

Lane is an arts educator, singer-songwriter, TEDx speaker, the president and founder of THREAD, and a long-time trailblazer in therapeutic arts. THREAD is a non-profit organization that brings the therapeutic power of creative expression to individuals and communities living in and with trauma. They serve the needs of survivors of abuse, those struggling with addiction and mental health, cancer survivors, incarcerated men and women, veterans, and those impacted by inequality and discrimination of all types. They also implement programs to address the urgent needs of communities affected by gun violence, natural disasters, and other crisis scenarios.

Lane's story starts in early childhood, around the age of four. Her mother was a talented pianist, and her father was a Vietnam veteran who had PTSD with little to no support upon his return home. Unfortunately, within a year of her father's return, Lane's parents divorced, and her family fell apart.

Four-year-old Lane faced the challenge of healing from her parent's divorce and being uprooted from her home. Then, she watched her mother struggle continuously for years and fell victim to a religious cult when she was remarried to an abusive man. During this point in Lane's life, her young mind decided it was time to figure out a way to survive.

"At such an early age, I had to get scrappy about figuring out how to survive. My mother was a pianist, and I also had other generations in my family who were self-taught musicians, including my grandfather, aunts, and uncles. Even though I was in this challenging situation as a young person, I had this lifeline: my family came together regularly for musical jam sessions. I started to understand the power of music. These were self-taught musicians. It was about having fun, connecting, and being together. This transcended all the difficulties that we were experiencing."

This experience taught me that creativity and music could create connection, healing, and experience with people beyond words. After that, I started attending the local community theater, taking voice and acting lessons. That ended up being my escape from the challenging situations that I was in at home. That was a safe and protective space. It was a community where I could start discovering who I was and what my gifts and talents were.

Lane did this for the rest of her high school years and eventually became a professional singer-actor. It was her first career, and she continued her musical theater and classical voice studies at a conservatory. Throughout that time, she was comforted not only by the community and the safe space but by being able to live in somebody else's stories as an actress and singer. *"I was singing somebody else's songs and portraying a character that was somebody else's story. That got me through a lot of my younger years. It was an escape, a safety net, and a lifeline. I would say that the arts saved my life."*

Lane found acceptance, support, and community in these creative space. *"When you are in a creative space, rehearsing shows, learning songs, and playing characters together, there is an element where everybody is on the same team. It requires everyone to step in and be a part of creating not only this show, performance, or concert, but it requires that each person brings their creativity and open-heartedness to the process.*

The overarching experience was that we all could bring our authentic selves to the table because that is how you make good art. It's when people are communicating from a heartful and authentic place. There are times when I see an artist singing a song, performing a concert, or in a show on stage, and there is a moment sometimes where I feel the tears in my throat when you're watching them. That's when you can feel the heart and soul of that person. It is cellular, and you can feel it. The arts can help us know ourselves better and understand each other better. It creates an authentic human connection that isn't based on competition, just creation."

Lane and I discussed how the arts could support us in discovering our authentic selves. As she shared, *"It's a lifetime job to uncover the depths of your true self, unearthing all the layers piled on us from our families and society. You don't have to be a 'creative person' or an 'artist' to express yourself authentically. You do that by simply finding the deepest parts of you that are the most resonant, the most free, and the most aligned with you. That takes time and effort to do and find that."*

What Lane shared reminded me of freedom of expression, the ability to express ourselves without holding back, with no boundaries. When you freely express yourself, it resonates right from your soul. It is like your soul is singing, and you can bring all of the things that are inside out.

Lane believes her involvement in the arts kept her alive in her younger years. After having the experience with the arts that she did, Lane knew she needed to share the gift of expression and safety the arts gave her with others, so she began teaching.

Many of us stifle our creativity as we progress through our years, and Lane shared a way to reconnect with it. *"I was a voice teacher for years, and I discovered that most people don't breathe as well as they should. We're walking around with all kinds of stress in our bodies. Part of the process of singing, speaking, or creating comes from this experience of learning how to open up your breath and body. If you release some of this tension from daily stress, you can tap into parts of yourself that are more expressive. As an artist and somebody who helps others with creativity, I have discovered that we have to start at the center of our bodies to release our full expression.*

From there, you begin to free up your creative source, whatever that is. It could be singing, cooking, painting, or designing a new product. Creativity isn't just about being an artist; it is about tapping into your essence, your authentic being. It comes from the breath, the heart, and the connection between them."

On her teaching journey, Lane and her husband Pete worked with many groups; however, one incredible experience in 2018 stands out. *"We were asked to work with the students of Marjory Stoneman Douglas High School in Parkland, Florida, a few months after the horrific mass shooting there. I had this process that I had been developing for a long time. We brought this therapeutic collaborative songwriting process to that moment in time. We worked with a licensed music therapist and collaborated with her.*

It changed my life, and I know it changed the lives of the young people we worked with. When we got there, they were still feeling the trauma. They not only created this incredibly powerful work of art, but they transformed their trauma into something so beautiful that it continued to help them when they shared that song with the other students in their school; collective healing happened here. That changed me forever. I thought, 'This is it, isn't it?' It's the individual and the collective process here. The healing happened on two different levels."

This experience led her to start THREAD, which was designed to expand this way of working with people to heal trauma with creative expression.

"Trauma is so pervasive. Trauma is in all of us, whether it's an experience you had as a young person being bullied or the inequality you're dealing with because of your skin color or who you love. It doesn't matter what these experiences are. We all have them, and we all share them with a group of people who have a similar experience as us.

The arts can do that. It can deliver that individual and collective healing that creates a safe space and connection between our shared stories. The art form itself is a safe container for sharing. We are now at the point of just getting started with what we can do with this. I believe with all of my heart that this is one of the innovations we need in mental health to help us heal from the long-term trauma that we all have."

To dive in, you don't have to be a talented or practiced musician or artist. Music and art are mediums to bring what's trapped inside to the outside; these feelings and sensations are often more profound than words can express. Lane shared a personal lesson that resonated with me deeply and that I think many of us need to remember: *"Connection is the key, connection to ourselves, others, and the world around us.*

One of the biggest lessons I have learned and continue to learn daily is that I need connection and support. As much as I am passionate about bringing this kind of help to others, you are only as strong as the circles that you are in. I have become more self-compassionate over the years. I had to remove that superhuman strength expectation of myself. It made me feel so much more connected to myself and other people in my life. It has also made me realize that I need people as much as they need me, and we are all in this together. We're all here together and bring our unique gifts and talents to the table. We can create a very different experience as human beings."

In the face of adversity, Lane Gardner's story is a testament to the power of creative expression to heal and connect with others. Music and art became the lifelines she needed to overcome her trauma. Her experience highlights the potential within each of us to tap into our creativity and demonstrates the importance of letting go of fear and embracing our authentic selves. Lane's efforts with THREAD and her work as an arts educator have illuminated a path for countless others to heal from their traumas and find solace in the transformative power of creative expression. We must remember that connection, vulnerability, and authenticity can bring light out of the darkness, allowing us to heal ourselves and contribute to the collective healing of those around us.

April Rinne: Reshaping Our Relationship with Change

April Rinne embodies the idea of living purposefully without holding yourself too tightly to one path. She has developed a "portfolio career" driven by a desire to impact the world. So who is April? She is a World Economic Forum Young Global Leader who is ranked among the top 50 leading female futurists. She is a change navigator who helps individuals and organizations rethink and reshape their relationships with change, uncertainty, and a world of flux. And April is also the author of the brilliant book, *Flux: 8 Superpowers For Thriving In Constant Change.* April is a true testament to the idea of post-traumatic growth.

Think about when you were 20 years old. You had so much to learn, yet you felt so grown. It is a year of transformation for most people; it is a time for young adults to experience the world firsthand and make big life decisions. It's a time to cultivate friendships, enjoy the beauty life offers, and begin the journey to determine who you really are.

Unfortunately for my friend April, when she was 20 years old, she went through an unexpected and tragic transformation that started when she received a phone call from her sister. This phone call would change her entire life forever. During our conversation, April recounts that she and her sister did not have a close relationship at the time, so it was a bit strange when she saw her sister's name appear on her phone. She remembers vividly thinking that something was wrong. The news she heard was that her parents were killed in a car accident, leaving her and her sister alone.

"I was twenty years old, and suddenly, every single part of my life changed. The future I thought I was going to have flipped upside down, and

that was a flashpoint. There was the life before my parents died, and then there was the life after my parents died. I was still me, but everything changed, and I had to think about how to rebuild our family. How do I deal with my grief and anxiety? And what does this mean for my career?"

As quickly as you can flip a light switch, the plan April had for her life was gone. She was overseas at college, with little support and a distant relationship with her only sibling. As her mind began to race, she knew, *"I had to grow up, and I had to become self-sufficient fast."*

Young April still had so much to learn in life, and while trying to mourn her parents and determine the direction her life would take, she developed an *"irrational belief that I didn't have long to live."* As she tried to process what had just happened to her family and her life, she developed a belief that this could happen to her, even if she were healthy, *"I started to believe this could happen to anybody, which led me to make very different decisions about what matters and what doesn't."*

Preparing for a midlife crisis experience at 20 years old is something April was not ready for. Nevertheless, her new insight into life lit a fire inside her that encouraged her to ask the hard questions that most of us don't ask until much later in life. As April processed her grief over the loss of her parents, she started to wonder, *"What's the purpose of my life? Have I lived a life of meaning and fulfillment? Have I made the right choices or priorities?"*

Raising these questions so early on in life profoundly impacted how the rest of April's life unfolded. Over the past 25 years, she has thought about how this tragedy impacted her life and how vastly different things would be now if she did not lose her parents.

"Had I been three years younger or three years older? Three years younger, I still would have been at home, more or less a dependent. It would have been disruptive in a whole different way. Three years later, I would have already started some kind of career. I probably would have had to ask to take time off a job, but I was in college, where I was in this limbo. It felt like I was swinging between two branches. I asked myself, 'What do you want to change? Would I go to grad school? Would I grieve? Would I get a job? Would I travel?' It was this blank slate."

When thinking about her younger years, April remembers her parents teaching her to see the good in everyone, a lesson that would prove valuable as she navigated her new normal. April was fortunate to have never experienced death before her parents, had never attended a funeral, or even lost a pet. However, she quickly realized how lucky she was to have never been in the position to experience loss.

"I didn't know what death was viscerally, and then I went from 0 to 100. As much as anyone can prepare for what life has in store, I don't think many people prepare for one day going from having never been to a funeral to the next day, both of your parents are gone. It is like I jumped in at the deep end

without a life jacket but didn't have much choice, so I would learn how to tread water, swim, and ultimately jump off a diving board."

April remembers *"in the immediate aftermath thinking I will die tomorrow. Not that I was going to, but my brain was already there. That ended up being helpful in some ways to walk through that fire. I think this is due in some non-trivial part to my parents. It wasn't, 'If I were to die tomorrow, what does my ego need me to do today? What sounds fun to do now?' It was always, 'What does the world need me to do? How can I be of service to others? How can I put humanity at the center?'"*

April began to wonder, *"What do I do when I don't know what to do? Where do I start?"* and found that *"the core question that grounded me and allowed me to move forward goes back to this irrational fear that I had about not having long to live, but I would always ask, 'If I were to die tomorrow, what would the world need me to do today?'"*

April began to have a clear vision around the fact that *"We have all of these rights as humans with just the fact of being human, but if we peel back the layer of that onion with one more layer, none of us has the right to be here, to begin with. It's this sense of borrowed time. We have all of these rights once we exist, but the fact of our existence is such a miracle, a stroke of magic, and good luck was the part I never want to forget to be grateful for. I can talk about everything like rights, privileges, and responsibilities, but at a deeper level, the right to even be here isn't inherent in the human condition. It's a huge gift. I feel like that became clear in the last couple of years. That is how I want to live my life."*

When faced with trauma and the opportunity to grow, there are two ways to look at it; the negative and the positive. For April, that *"sense of what it means to explore your life, take risks, and recognize privilege"* pushed her toward a journey that has been anything but linear, marked by flashpoints that have shaped her personal and professional development. The tragedy of losing her parents early in life catalyzed April's pursuit of meaning and purpose. She defied societal expectations and chose her own path, curating her unique career portfolio.

After her parents' death, April faced the challenge of stepping into the world without a blueprint. When presented with the opportunity to work at an investment bank or consulting firm, instead, she followed her heart, guiding hiking and biking trips around the world. This decision earned her the criticism of her peers and mentors, but she remained undeterred. Her experiences traveling and connecting with people of different cultures became her true North, guiding her professional decisions. Her portfolio led her through various roles, including a stint in law school and pursuing atypical opportunities. Ultimately, those who had previously questioned her choices sought guidance on following a similar path. This validation, though not sought, solidified April's belief in the value of forging your unique life path.

Another interesting aspect of her travels is her handstands. She has done handstands all around the world, and she shared this wonderful wisdom: *"When you stand on your hands or do any kind of inversion, you see the same things, but you see them differently. It is a totally fresh perspective."* What began as a playful challenge from her friends and family evolved into a powerful icebreaker during her travels. The handstands allowed April to connect with locals and experience the world in a more intimate way, reinforcing her belief in the goodness of humanity.

April Rinne's immense loss at the age of 20 served as a significant flashpoint from which she emerged stronger and more purpose-driven. Her journey epitomizes the concept of post-traumatic growth, where adversity fuels personal evolution and a deeper understanding of the world. Through her unique approach to life, embracing change and uncertainty, she has built a meaningful and impactful career that touches the lives of countless individuals and organizations.

April's story is a powerful reminder that from the darkest moments in our lives, we can emerge enlightened, resilient, and inspired to make a difference from the darkest moments in our lives. In embracing our own unique paths and seeking purpose in the face of adversity, we too can manifest light from darkness and contribute positively to the world around us.

The Lessons

The theme "Out of Darkness Comes the Light" holds immense significance in our lives and society as a whole. It is a reminder that even in the bleakest of moments, there is always a glimmer of hope. The concept highlights that adversity can lead to growth and that through our struggles and hardships, we can find the strength and resilience to overcome them and emerge stronger and wiser.

Ann Brennan's story is one of strength, resilience, and the power of vulnerability. After experiencing the darkness of her son's mental health struggles and her own decline into hopelessness and suicidal thoughts, Ann found the courage to ask for help and share her story. Through her non-profit organization, she raises money and awareness for suicide prevention, and through her digital marketing company and podcast, she created a platform to help others tell their stories. Ann's journey shows that by being brave enough to share our darkest moments and ask for help, we can emerge from the shadows and bring light to both ourselves and others. The power of connection and honest conversation can illuminate the lives of those around us.

Lane Gardner's story is a beautiful example of how creative expression through art can help individuals heal from trauma. Lane has witnessed the transformative power of creative expression firsthand as a singer-songwriter and founder of THREAD, a non-profit organization that brings therapeutic arts to individuals and communities living with trauma. Her experience highlights the potential within each of us to tap into our creativity and demonstrates the importance of letting go of fear and embracing our authentic selves. Lane's efforts have illuminated a path for countless others to heal from their traumas and find solace in the transformative power of creative expression.

April Rinne has developed a "portfolio career" driven by a desire to impact the world. Her life journey began with a traumatic event at 20 years old when she lost her parents in a car accident while studying abroad. Despite the loss and grief, she found the strength to rebuild her life and redefine her purpose. She developed an irrational belief that she didn't have long to live, encouraging her to ask the hard questions that most of us don't ask until much later in life. Her story epitomizes post-traumatic growth. April's unique approach to life, embracing change and uncertainty, has enabled her to build a meaningful and impactful career that touches the lives of countless individuals and organizations.

Questions

As we wrap up this lesson, let's circle back to the three C's of grounded leadership: curiosity, compassion, and connection, with some questions for you to ponder and journal.

- How can you use the skills, knowledge, and experience you have gained to serve others?
- We have seen several mentions of the importance of connection when trying to come out of the darkness. Who do you turn to when things get dark for you?
- How do you spark your curiosity and look for the lesson when facing a difficult situation?
- When have you shared something personal with someone and created a deeper connection?

End Notes

"People develop new understandings of themselves, the world they live in, how to relate to other people, the kind of future they might have, and a better understanding of how to live life." Tedeschi, Richard G. & Calhoun, Lawrence G. *Trauma & Transformation: Growing in the Aftermath of Suffering* SAGE Publications, 1995.
Emotional Intelligence 2.0 – Travis Bradberry and Jean Greaves
Flux: 8 Superpowers for Thriving in Constant Change – April Rinne

Lesson 3

Embrace Emotional Courage

In my first book, *Climbing the Right Mountain: Navigating the Journey to an Inspired Life*, I spoke about my journey of leaving the corporate world to become a coach and an entrepreneur. I knew I had to have the emotional courage to explore deeper and answer the questions I was afraid to answer.

But what does emotional courage really mean? Emotional courage means acknowledging and welcoming emotions that may be uncomfortable to explore. For instance, many people may avoid trying something new because they fear it will jeopardize their reputation if they fail. Therefore, they will do anything to avoid looking foolish or experiencing embarrassment. However, emotional courage will require you to embrace fear and let it drive you forward regardless of the emotional consequences. The same is true for positive emotions; accepting and pursuing happiness can also feel risky.

Nevertheless, being emotionally courageous can be the key to unlocking a better version of yourself. Rather than avoiding difficult feelings, open your heart and mind by leaning into both good and bad emotions; this can liberate you from them in unexpected ways, creating space for more informed decisions and greater fulfillment.

As you will see, emotional courage is a superpower anyone can tap into. When you broaden your emotional range, you become more resilient and adaptable in the face of new challenges. Expanding your capacity to experience emotions skillfully and gracefully will ultimately allow you to live a more fulfilling life.

How does emotional courage relate to the three C's of grounded leadership: curiosity, compassion, and connection? Well, let's start with curiosity. Get curious about your emotions; what are they trying to tell you in these moments that you might need to listen to? Are they trying to keep you safe or holding you back from an experience that will help you grow?

From a compassionate perspective, we must first express that it is okay to have challenging emotions; it's just part of the human experience. But

DOI: 10.4324/9781003364818-4

why are you feeling this way, and how can you get support to navigate these emotions?

This leads to connection. We don't have to take the emotional leap alone. Look for help from others who can guide you on this path, even if it is simply to create a space to express your thoughts and feelings.

Embracing emotional courage looks different for everyone. Some people jump in with both feet, hoping to land on solid ground. Others like to dip their feet into the water slowly. You can inch down the beach even if you are not ready to jump into the water. There is no right or wrong way to move forward; the simple act of forward movement builds courage.

When I think about my story, I faced many emotional challenges when I left a safe corporate job to start my coaching business. My worries kept piling up: What would people think of me? Where would I start? What if I fail? How will I support my family? These were not easy things to overcome, but I also worried about not living my life fully if I stayed in my current situation. Something was missing in the workplace that I could create through my unique contribution, so I had to do something about it. I held on to Peter Bregman's quote: "If you're willing to feel everything, you can have anything." So I made the conscious choice not to hold myself back, to leap into the unknown and give myself a shot at experiencing the life I wanted.

Emotional courage also allows you to broaden your range and your resilience. In challenging moments, we discover what we are capable of and often discover our hidden potential. Even failure can be translated into learning. This is where the practice of self-compassion comes in. If we move forward with emotional courage, we permit ourselves to move forward as quickly or as slowly as we are comfortable. We embrace what we learned and grow more resilient when we can bravely keep moving forward, no matter what.

Imposter syndrome comes up for many of us on the edge of taking a giant leap. We may ask ourselves, "Who am I to do this?" or "Am I qualified to do this?" Imposter syndrome can stymie anyone – including experts, professionals, and literal geniuses. Most of us feel these feelings at some point. We may struggle with feeling worthiness. These feelings are normal, and most people experience them throughout their entire lives, especially those willing to step forward with emotional courage. I often say that imposter syndrome is not a flaw but a feature. It tells us that we are on the right track because we are moving into a growth stage.

An exercise that I continue to go back to when faced with situations that require emotional courage is to weigh out the possibilities before I get clear on what outcomes I'm okay with. I ask myself these questions:

- What could be the best outcome?
- What might be the worst outcome?

- What is the most likely outcome?
- What are some potential obstacles, and how might I deal with them?
- What is my current risk tolerance?
- What would I be okay with letting go of, and what do I have to gain?
- Finally, what small steps or giant leaps would propel me forward?

These questions can help you decide what to do next and create a plan to get started. You may not be ready to quit your job and move across the country to start your dream job as a scuba diving instructor; however, you may be prepared to sign up for your first scuba diving lesson. Emotional courage does not necessarily mean you are leaping blindly into the unknown. Instead, we can chart our expected course and decide what pace we would like to proceed.

Recently, I reflected on the idea that sitting in discomfort is a good thing, as you will read in the stories in this chapter. If we always got what we wanted immediately, without challenge or obstacles, we would experience no joy in attaining it. Would it still feel rewarding if our journey through life was easy? On the contrary, we value things more when overcoming adversity to achieve them. That is why the view at the top of a mountain can be breathtaking after a challenging climb. Experiencing challenges helps us prepare to move forward. It broadens our range of what is possible and reminds us, once again, that we are resilient people who can meet our challenges head-on and survive each and every one.

Emotional courage is the gateway to living a fulfilling life, so let's dive into stories of people who embody emotional courage by learning from past trauma and using their experiences to help others. Through their journeys, we will gain a deeper understanding of what it means to have emotional courage and how it can change our lives.

Peter Bregman: Emotional Courage and Embracing Discomfort

Peter Bregman literally wrote the book on emotional courage. He has written a few fantastic books, but the one that impacted me the most was *Leading With Emotional Courage*, one of my favorite books. So I was honored and thrilled to connect with Peter. I felt like I was meeting one of my heroes when I had him join me on *The Virtual Campfire*. And it was a privilege to uncover his story.

We talked about how change is uncomfortable, but it is also inevitable. Without change, we can't move forward. So what can we do to not only be comfortable with change, but also make the most out of it? Peter shared the flashpoints in his life that helped him be comfortable with change and ultimately achieve the success and impact he has today.

Recognized as the #1 executive coach in the world by Leading Global Coaches, Peter Bregman coaches C-Level executives in many of the world's premier organizations. Peter is also the host of the *Bregman Leadership Podcast* and a regular contributor to the Harvard Business Review. In addition, his articles and commentary frequently appear in Bloomberg, BusinessWeek, Fast Company, Psychology Today, Forbes, The Financial Times, PBS, ABC, CNN, NPR, and FOX Business News.

Peter's first flashpoint, interestingly enough, started before he was born: *"The first thing that comes to mind is my Jewish heritage. My mother is French, and during the Holocaust, she was in hiding in France near the Swiss border. Her family tried to get over the Swiss border, but couldn't so they spent the rest of the war in a place called Annecy.*

For me, the stories of the Holocaust, perhaps even the ancestral energetic formation of who I am in the context of my mother's experiences in the Holocaust, are foundational. There are all sorts of things that determine and change our lives. For many of us, it is experienced before we are even alive. The experience of the Holocaust was present in my life growing up and continues to be in many ways.

My mother's experiences influenced me, and she was formed by the experiences her parents had. We are not a tabula rasa. We come from somewhere and make many choices, but where we come from generally is not a choice. What we do with that is a choice."

Throughout high school and into college, Peter followed his passion for politics. As a junior in high school, he even worked for the Senate Democratic Policy Committee and wrote the Democratic Policy Approach to Nicaragua and El Salvador. Years later, as a student at Princeton University, Peter found himself wrestling with this chosen path. Feeling disillusioned, he decided to change course and study in France. His father shared this wisdom with him: *'If there is something specific you want to learn, great. I will support you. We'll figure out how you can go to France. But, if you are doing it because you are bored at Princeton and don't know what else to do or don't know what your next move is, you will face that for the rest of your life. So, figure out where you are. Don't run from it.' It was terrific advice, which I followed.'"*

Leaving his previous dream of working in politics behind wasn't easy, but it taught him valuable lessons about honoring himself and the value of taking a courageous leap.

"I wasn't learning. I decided to prioritize my own experience of learning. I didn't want to just fight the fight for the rest of my life. I didn't want to stand for something so firmly that I couldn't learn and listen to the other side. More than anything, I value learning and growth. I don't always enjoy being wrong, but I'm open to being wrong. I love ideas, and I love learning.

In some ways, there are moments that you walk away from and then moments that you walk towards.

The scary part of the transition is the ambiguity in the middle. I can be clear about walking away from something without knowing or being clear about what I'm walking towards. That's scary. It's like letting go of an unknown and grasping for ambiguity. That's a hard move to make. The tricky part of change is letting go of something you know to move towards something you don't."

He shares, *"As you think about a change you might make, you must talk about being uncomfortable. In my book,* Leading with Emotional Courage, *you must be willing to feel the risk if you want to make a move. You have to be willing to feel that this may be the wrong decision.*

You don't know because we know very little about the future. You have to be willing to take risks to create something new. If you're waiting to make a change until you know with 100% certainty that you're right, you'll never make the change because, by definition, you're leaving the past for a future. The past is always 100% certain, and the future is never 100% certain."

Along his journey, Peter became a National Outdoor Leadership School (NOLS) and an Outward Bound instructor. He spent months at a time in the woods and loved it. After considering other career paths, he eventually settled on opening his own business teaching leadership in corporations and was ultimately tapped to join a company focused on transformational organizational change. Today, he is the Founder and CEO of Bregman Partners, helping successful people become exceptional leaders and stellar human beings.

"I have a low tolerance for boredom, making it hard to scale my company because I want to do different things. It keeps me learning, but it also has challenges. I have tried many different things, and the failures reflect success because it reflects an attempt at doing something. Unfortunately, there are too many people who don't even try. To me, it is all about putting yourself out there.

That's the reality of taking a risk and putting yourself out there. You're going to get blowback. People are going to hate you, and they're going to love you. Don't get swayed by either one. Stay the course of what you're trying to learn, how you're trying to grow, and the impact you're trying to make, and then all this other stuff will be noise."

Peter Bregman's story is one of resilience and transformation, where he has turned his uncomfortable experiences into a source of strength. Peter's Jewish heritage and his mother's experiences during the Holocaust played a significant role in shaping his worldview. Through his struggles with finding his path in life, Peter learned that the discomfort of change is a necessary part of growth. His willingness to take risks and embrace uncertainty has led him to make a huge impact in the world. Peter's journey highlights the importance of honoring yourself and taking courageous leaps, even if you don't know where they will lead. He reminds us that we all can create opportunities for growth and expansion and that fear should not hold us back.

Nancy Barrows: Unleashing the Brave Space Within

Nancy Barrows is truly a brave voice in the world. She is committed to sharing her story, speaking openly and honestly, and showing up authentically, and she invites others to join her in creating a *Brave Space* where everyone can be themselves and receive the unconditional love and acceptance they deserve. Nancy works to disarm the stigma and remove our "invisible report cards," which she explains make us too uncomfortable to engage in powerful, transformative conversations. She believes our most authentic selves are revealed by removing the stigma and "social masks" that hold us back. By actively fostering a *Brave Space* where difficult conversations can happen, she works to change lives and culture.

Nancy is a community creator and gatherer who is often called "The Queen of Engagement." She is the producer and host of the weekly show *Connected Human Conversations*, founder of the #RadiatingReal movement, and creator of *The Chick With the Toolbelt* program. As a keynote speaker, she aims to inspire and help others discover their true selves by taking off the "social masks" they wear and showing up authentically.

When life gets you down or makes you angry, remember that these emotions will pass. There is a beautiful life for you out there despite the setbacks you have encountered. Nancy is passionate about helping people find what is already inside them and offering it to the world. She shared her journey of experiencing abuse at a young age. For the longest time, Nancy believed she was broken beyond repair and that there was no way to fix her life. However, she eventually found a way to heal and bounce back from her challenges.

Her story starts with how she learned the power of vulnerability and how this vulnerability led her to create a brave space for others.

"I didn't realize that that's what they were until I was beyond my flashpoints. They were catalysts for my growth and for what would come next. My first one was when I was about 15 years old, so I invite your readers to receive my story without judgment; it is not an easy story to receive. It's not something that's often talked about. I certainly do not have any judgment of them for any reaction they have. I have probably had them myself.

At fifteen years old, I was at a summer program. A bunch of young girls were talking, and I suddenly got upset. One brave girl asked me what was wrong, and she caught me in a moment. I shared with her that my grandfather had been sexually abusing me since I was about 4 or 5 years old. The girl didn't know what to do with this information, so she went to an adult in the program who was a mandated reporter. I didn't even know there were laws against what was going on.

Here is the secret that I carefully kept because, in my mind, my life depended on it. The secret was unleashed. I use that word intentionally. It was unleashed on my family. It was this wave that went across everyone.

Even then, I didn't realize that when you go through things, the people around you also go through them. I didn't get it until I was older that my mom and dad had to process what had happened to their daughter and watch her go through it. My mom was dealing with the news of what her father had done, so she was processing that, too. There are so many pieces of the journey that I later came to appreciate. So that started what doesn't sound like, at first, a healing journey."

Nancy shares so frankly about all aspects of her journey because she wants to ensure that when people reflect on their journeys, they understand that healing is a messy process.

"I am all about talking about the ugly, snotty, and unsexy moments in the journey because that's important. We don't want to leave anyone seeing the end of the story and thinking they're failing because we have these internal report cards like, 'She's out there speaking about it, and she's doing great. She's healthy and recovered, but I'm not getting out of bed for three days. I'm not showering.' I was there, too. So it's important that they watch me go through all of that."

Her story continues with the challenges after her secret was "unleashed" and the turns her life took as she navigated her journey.

"I became anorexic. For me, it was about hating and punishing my body. In my mind, my body was broken beyond repair, and it had betrayed me. Another hard thing for people to hear, especially those who have been through abuse, is that every cell in my body was programmed to do precisely what it did. It worked beautifully. Sexual touch equals pleasure. Only I didn't want it. That was all rewired, all crossed, and all mixed up. My body had betrayed me, so why would I give it nutrition? Why provide it with sustenance? Why treat it well? I hated it, and I wanted to disappear.

Beyond a shadow of a doubt, I believed I was broken beyond repair. There was no fixing me."

Therapy became an excellent tool for her to unpack what was happening in her life. She was also grateful and fortunate to have her family's support as she navigated this confusing and unsettling period. Finally, at 20 years old, she confronted her grandfather, leading to her next major flashpoint.

Nancy shared, *"I had gotten to the point where through therapy, I knew it wasn't my fault. I had not done anything wrong. But I wanted somebody to take responsibility for my pain. In my mind, this was going to be my ticket to freedom. But unfortunately, not every story goes the way you think it's going to go. So I went and confronted my grandfather. He admitted to one instance where he had been inappropriate with me. So instead of being the ticket to freedom, it was devastating.*

Someone took responsibility for it, but everything I was dealing with didn't disappear. I didn't get to hand over the trauma with the responsibility. It was still all mine. He didn't have to go to therapy for it. I had to go to therapy, do the work, roll up my sleeves, roll around in the mud, and do that work, even though I had done nothing wrong, and it wasn't my fault. That led to my first major depressive episode, and I dropped out of college.

I have worn many different masks throughout my life. I had the high school mask, where I was the president of my class, captain of my volleyball team, and socially popular. Moving on to college, I'd gotten into this prestigious five-year undergrad Master's program in Speech-Language Pathology. How was I dropping out? I had only been there for two years. My ego would not allow me to say I couldn't hack it academically, and it did not fit with the mask I had formed with the people I was wearing. But ultimately, it didn't matter because I stayed in bed most of the time and had to drop out.

My brother lived in Los Angeles, and I was still in New York, and we conceived this idea that I would come to LA and do a summer session at UCLA where I could live in the dorms, take a class, and have some free time on my own. I like to call it my 'trial life.' My brother was my safety net because he was just 15 minutes away from campus. I had the best summer of my life. I'm not a drinker, but the pain had become so great that I used drinking and partying as the perfect mask."

What Nancy presented on the outside couldn't be more different from what was happening inside. She began to realize that you can't outrun your story. She started to have gratitude for it all and went from trying to outrun her story to inviting it to walk with her because there was so much value in what she had been through.

At some point, you have to face your past and use it to move forward. If you continue to avoid it, it will control you and hold you back from living fully. It is humbling to imagine how much pain Nancy had to endure to rehash the past repeatedly and relive those past experiences until she found a place to begin healing. But it is also a great testament to her bravery.

"To leave it behind or try to outrun it would be a disservice to me and anyone else that comes into my life because I can share what I share and do what I do because of what I've been through. It was painful, but I have learned by going through what I have gone through that it doesn't have to remain painful every day.

I realized I was a survivor and wore it for a long time as a badge of honor. However, I was an angry and tough survivor, saying, 'Bring it on! Come at me! I can take it!' That's true about a lot of us that go through trauma. For me, it felt stronger to be angry than vulnerable. It's funny because I have heard from people who came across me then who told me they were intimidated by me."

One way Nancy created a shift for herself was to have relationships where she felt safe putting down her carefully constructed mask and practicing being on the receiving end of radical acceptance. For example, Nancy shared, *"I met these three incredible women when I came to UCLA that gave me life. These were the first three people with whom I chose to take my mask off, and they didn't see me any differently. They didn't run or look at me with pity. What they did do was offer me unconditional love and acceptance."*

After her divorce, Nancy decided it was time to be 100% real, 100% of the time. She had been afraid of dropping the mask entirely, but now she realized, *"I want to be real, but more importantly, I need to be real, not just for me, but for other people, too. And that decision has been reinforced whenever someone comes up to me and says, 'Your story inspired me. You are so brave.' I have had countless men and women hear me speak, contact me, or walk up to me and tell me their stories. So often, it's the first time. It gives me chills just thinking about the privilege I have of being in that moment with them."*

One of the things that stuck out about our conversation was when she brought up the masks. So many people are carrying around their own masks to try and protect themselves. But they realize they are holding themselves back from being their true selves by putting a boundary between themselves and the world. Also, when you get into an environment with people who give you that sense of "I can be me here," it makes all the difference.

She went on to talk about her experiences in therapy and how something as simple as arranging the furniture in her therapist's office helped her feel safe enough to open up and share honestly. Finding safe spaces and safe people to be vulnerable set her on a healing path, where she could start digging into those deeper layers with honesty, self-compassion, and vulnerability.

"When you show up and are real, your tribe finds you. You can recognize each other. Your people are present and willing to step forward instead of step back when things get ugly, hairy, and dicey, lifting you up, celebrating you, and celebrating with you."

Nancy Barrows is a brave voice in the world who invites others to join her in creating a space where everyone can be themselves and receive the unconditional love and acceptance they deserve. Through sharing her journey of experiencing abuse at a young age, Nancy works to disarm the stigmas that hold us back from engaging in powerful, transformative conversations. Her story of learning the power of vulnerability and creating a Brave Space for others is a testament to the healing power of authenticity and vulnerability. Nancy's journey reminds us that healing is a messy process, but we can create a life filled with authenticity and joy by facing our past and using it to move forward. By actively fostering a Brave Space where difficult conversations can happen, Nancy works to change lives and culture, inviting us all to unleash the Brave Space within ourselves.

The Lessons

We have explored the concept of emotional courage and how it relates to various aspects of our lives, from personal growth to professional success. We have heard stories of individuals who have taken risks, faced adversity, and embraced their true selves with courage and resilience. Through these stories, we see that emotional courage is not about being fearless but about facing our fears and vulnerabilities with grace and determination. It is about being true to ourselves, showing up authentically, and inspiring others to do the same. As we move forward, we can be mindful of cultivating emotional courage in our own lives.

Through Peter Bregman's struggles with finding his path in life, he learned that discomfort is a necessary part of growth. The idea of really leaning into uncomfortable emotions, especially during the ambiguity in the middle of the transition, was so impactful to me. Understanding that you don't know what's really on the other side, but taking the leap anyway can feel intimidating and downright terrifying. However, I love that Peter stresses the importance of feeling whatever comes with the journey, good and bad, ups and downs, in order to have the full experience of living.

Nancy Barrow's journey reminds us that healing is a messy process, but we can create a life filled with authenticity and joy by facing our past and using it to move forward. We, too, can work to foster spaces where difficult conversations can happen, where people can remove their masks and lean into their own authenticity. Unleashing our true selves can feel uncomfortable, but we truly can find our tribe when we are able to let go of who we think we are supposed to be. There is so much power in removing our own masks, being vulnerable, and enjoying a life that comes with being authentically ourselves.

Questions

As we wrap up Lesson 3, let's circle back to the three C's of grounded leadership: curiosity, compassion, and connection, with some questions for you to ponder and journal.

- How have you been holding yourself back from taking risks or pursuing your dreams because of fear or self-doubt?
- Who are some role models in your life who have demonstrated emotional courage, and what can you learn from their examples?
- How can you use your unique talents and strengths to positively impact your community or the world?
- What is one courageous step you can take today to move closer to your goals and live a more fulfilling life?

End Notes

Climbing the Right Mountain – Tony Martignetti
Leading with Emotional Courage – Peter Bregman

Failing Forward

The Art of Navigating Setbacks

How do we deal with failure? This chapter will delve into the crucial lesson that accepting setbacks and failures is a natural part of growth. Unfortunately, we live in a world where success often equates with perfection, where every mistake is seen as a weakness. However, this mindset only stifles our progress and prevents us from reaching our full potential. It's time to reject the notion that failure is a negative thing and embrace it as a necessary part of our journey.

The concept of "failing forward" involves using failures as opportunities for growth and learning. This lesson is vital in today's fast-paced world, where the pressure to succeed can be overwhelming. But it's important to remember that failure is not the end, it's just a detour on the road to success. We will dive into stories of successful individuals who have faced setbacks and failures and how they used those experiences to push themselves forward to reach their goals.

As I shared in Lesson 1, a growth mindset is essential. When you adopt a growth mindset, you see failures as opportunities to learn rather than an indication of your abilities. It provides a framework for failing forward because it prescribes embracing challenges and persistence through obstacles. For example, when you make a mistake, don't let it paralyze you. Instead, analyze what went wrong and use that knowledge to improve your future performance.

Another key element of failing forward is experimentation. Try new things and test different approaches to achieve your goals. This involves taking risks and being willing to fail in pursuing learning and growth. Experimentation is critical to failing forward because it allows you to explore new ideas. It opens up new possibilities and helps you to think outside the box. When you experiment, you identify what works and what doesn't, test out different approaches, and learn from your successes and failures.

When you have a growth mindset and embrace experimentation, you become more resilient in the face of failure. You don't see failure as a dead

DOI: 10.4324/9781003364818-5

end but rather as a stepping stone to success. You understand that failure is an inevitable part of the learning process and that taking risks and trying new things to grow is necessary. So, the next time you encounter a setback, embrace a growth mindset and experiment to fail forward.

How does failing forward relate to the three C's of grounded leadership: curiosity, compassion, and connection? Failing forward involves connecting with yourself and your goals by recognizing that setbacks and failures are a natural part of growth. By embracing failure as a necessary part of the journey, you cultivate self-compassion and self-awareness, acknowledging that mistakes and failures do not define you.

Regarding curiosity, failing forward involves being open to learning and experimentation. You can give yourself permission to explore new ideas, test different approaches, and learn from the results. Curiosity helps us overcome self-pity or staying stuck in our own disappointment. We can find our course when we get curious about what happened, what could have gone differently, what to focus on next, and what opportunities now lie before us. Failure does not reflect who we are, how skilled we are at any given thing, or our capacity to learn. It simply indicates that it's time to get curious.

Finally, having compassion for yourself allows you to stay focused on your goals, maintain a positive attitude, and persevere through setbacks. Failure is just learning in action, and reframing "failure" and "continuous learning" is the compassionate approach as you find your way forward.

When we talk about taking risks, failing forward has to do with connecting to the idea that nothing ventured means nothing gained. In other words, to achieve great things, we must take chances, and sometimes that might fail. But failure doesn't have to be the end of the road. Instead, it can be a learning opportunity or a chance to adjust our plans and try again.

Measuring risk is essential to this process. Many of us want to take risks, but don't want to risk everything. Taking a measured risk involves being intentional and thinking through the potential outcomes before taking action. We can create a sense of safety while still being willing to move forward.

Risk is often discussed in the finance world, and for a good reason. In order to ensure we are taking risks on our own terms, we need to understand our level of risk tolerance and what we are willing to risk. We can't risk too much, or we might find ourselves overexposed and unable to come back from it.

The Startup of You, a book by Reid Hoffman, co-founder of LinkedIn, and Ben Casnocha, co-founder of Village Global, introduces the concept of plan A, plan B, and plan Z. Plan A is what we want to see happen, plan B is something we always have in the back of our minds, and plan Z is the absolute worst-case scenario. Understanding all of the potential outcomes can help us feel more secure in taking risks, knowing that we have backup plans in place.

We also need to be comfortable with the level of risk we are taking. Some people are okay with going all in, while others need more safety nets. However you choose to move forward, the important part is the willingness. You can choose your risk tolerance, have backup plans, stumble along the way, and consequently achieve great success.

Are you ready to be inspired? Let's explore the stories of incredible individuals who have embraced the power of failing forward. Although they have stumbled and faced adversity, they have used their setbacks as fuel to reach greater heights. They have many lessons to share about how failure can actually lead to growth and success.

Laura Gassner Otting: How to Achieve Limitless Possibility

Laura Gassner Otting is a powerhouse. She is someone who, once you meet her, you won't likely forget her. She has a lasting impact on you because she makes you feel like anything is possible and that you are limitless.

For the past 25 years, Laura Gassner Otting has dedicated her time to studying leaders and guiding them through pivotal moments in their personal and professional lives. With experience as a political appointee during Bill Clinton's presidency and as the founder and president of a global executive search company, her insights are unrivaled. Her book, *Limitless: How to Ignore Everybody, Carve Your Own Path, and Live Your Best Life*, was a critical and commercial success. Robin Roberts named it one of her favorite books of the year. Not only that, but she has also contributed regularly to The TODAY Show, Good Morning America, and Harvard Business Review. She is also the author of the recently released, *Wonderhell: Why Success Doesn't Feel Like It Should... ... and What to Do About It.*

Laura collaborates with change agents, entrepreneurs, investors, leaders, and donors to push past the doubt and indecision that consign great ideas to limbo. She helps people get unstuck and achieve extraordinary results through limitless possibilities. She supports people by delivering strategic thinking, well-honed wisdom, and a catalytic perspective informed by decades of navigating change across the startup, non-profit, political, and philanthropic landscape. As I said, she is a powerhouse.

One of Laura's key flashpoints was when she ran into the then-governor, Bill Clinton, at his campaign office in a tiny strip mall in Gainesville, Florida. She remembers him talking about being of service. He said, "There is nothing wrong with America that can't be fixed with what is right with America," and she was immediately sold on the idea that she could be of service. In my conversation with Laura, it was clear that she has strong values, prioritizes fairness, and enables people to serve in a way that will help us move forward as a society. As we explored Laura's journey, I was reminded of the quote from Mahatma Gandhi, "The best way to find yourself is to lose yourself in the service of others."

Laura shared, *"I believe you lose yourself in that process, but you also find yourself. For example, I finished a three-year study on what makes people happy at work. It's all based on the work I did in recruiting and the book I wrote, Limitless. In the book, I talk about the idea of consonance, where it's not the pursuit of happiness or success; it's the pursuit of consonance."*

This concept refers to the alignment between who you are and what you do in the world. When there is consonance, you feel a sense of purpose, fulfillment, and joy in your work and life. Consonance has four components: calling, connection, contribution, and control.

- Calling is the gravitational force that gets you out of bed in the morning, the inspiration to build a business, grow the bottom line, nurture your family, solve a problem, or whatever it is.
- Connection is about whether your work connects to that calling. Are you connected? Does what's on your calendar or your to-do list matter? Does it get you closer to your calling?
- Contribution is about building the life that you want. Does this work contribute to your ability to manifest your values daily, to have the career trajectory you want and lifestyle you want to live?
- Control is about how much agency you have to affect the projects you are working on or the teams assigned to you. How is your work judged, and how are you rewarded for it?

During Laura's study, she noticed something really interesting. One would assume that post-pandemic, we would have much less control; however, *"I found that most of these metrics, calling, connection, and contribution, stayed the same, but we've all got more control."* Interestingly, the pandemic brought forth some insightful questions for many people, Laura included. People started questioning whether the life they would return to was the one they wanted. In the uncertainty of the pandemic, many people found the clarity they desperately needed and are now on track to being who they are meant to be.

Laura is an avid runner and rower, both exceptionally challenging sports. She recalls the first marathon she ever ran and entered what athletes call the pain cave – a place where you learn what you are made of when things get hard. As Laura worked her mind and body to finish the marathon she committed to, she realized *"the pain cave it's not a cave. It's a tunnel, and you can come out the other side. When you come out the other side, you say, 'I'm made of more than I thought. I learned something about myself in this place. The next time I go there, I can go a little farther.'"*

This ability to be comfortable with being uncomfortable makes a huge difference. When we don't know where we are going, or when we feel completely out of control, those are the moments where we need to return to our fundamental state of inner leadership.

When we understand the importance of discovering our true purpose and pursuing it fearlessly, we can break free from our limiting beliefs and create a life aligned with our values and passions.

"Who are you when you are at your very best? You are firing on all cylinders, making it rain, and closing the deal. Maybe you are having this quiet moment with a loved one. You are helping a colleague through a hard situation. You are in this moment where you can walk through fire. You can leap over tall buildings. You are at your fundamental best. In these moments, if you practice being that person, you can find that person deep at the bottom of your pain cave and go into it."

Years ago, Laura had the opportunity to speak at Camp Zama, an Army base in Japan. While there, she trained alongside those stationed at the base and learned to do an exercise called the hollow hold. Laura caught on quickly, and before she knew it was competing directly with one young guy who was left holding his hollow hold. She remembers watching the expression on his face fade away and wondering if he was okay. Then, within just a moment, he came back more motivated than ever to beat her.

"He could hold on for a half-hour if he had to. I don't know what kind of training he had, but he knew that he had to get to that place where he was comfortable being uncomfortable. He did it. I looked at him. Fifteen seconds later, I dropped my arms and legs. I told myself, 'It doesn't matter how long I hold it. I'm not beating him. He figured out how to be comfortable with being uncomfortable.'"

Laura admits she has done several things in her professional life that have made those around her, those that love her, question what she was doing. Sometimes the voices of her past have taken over and made her wonder if she could find the success she was looking for. But, in those dark moments in her pain cave, she reminds herself, *"You have survived all your bad days. You have survived all of your failures. There's a track record there. You are going to survive."*

During her impressive career, one of the most critical lessons Laura has learned is *"Failure is not the finale. Very few of us are failures in the end. Instead, we have to learn how to get comfortable with being uncomfortable. Sometimes that means stepping out and doing things you can't always do perfectly the first time. As a kid, I never wanted to try anything I couldn't do the first time perfectly. I was the typical kid who sat on the sidelines until I knew I could master something, then I would do it perfectly because I had to be perfect. That's who I was. That was my identity. I have gotten much older and more mature. Now, I am totally fine sucking at something new."*

There are always going to be times in life when we fail. However, when we focus on the lessons involved in failure, we can learn and grow from them. Most importantly, in the moments that your pain cave feels endless, remember *"failure is not fatal."*

Laura Gassner Otting is an inspiring force who has dedicated her life to helping others find alignment in their work and personal lives. By aligning her values with her work, Laura has found that pursuing consonance has been key to her success. Her ability to be comfortable with being uncomfortable has helped her navigate the most challenging situations. She understands that failure is not fatal and that we should focus on the lessons learned from it. I love that through her work, she encourages others to embrace their passions and overcome their limiting beliefs to create lives that align with their values.

Todd Cherches: The Power of Visual Leadership

Visual thinking is a powerful tool for solving problems, unlocking creativity, and making connections we might not see otherwise. Todd Cherches is a master of visual thinking, among many things. When I met Todd, I immediately noticed his insightfulness, witty sense of humor, and down-to-earth humility. I have been a huge fan ever since, and I continue to be amazed at his ability to see things that others might overlook and how he uses these gifts to help others.

Todd is the CEO and co-founder of BigBlueGumball, a New York City-based management consulting firm specializing in leadership development, public speaking, and executive coaching. He's also a three-time award-winning adjunct professor of leadership at NYU, a lecturer on leadership at Columbia University, and a TEDx speaker. He's the author of *VisuaLeadership: Leveraging the Power of Visual Thinking in Leadership and in Life.*

Interestingly enough, Todd considers himself an extreme introvert and describes himself as *"a '3 B's' kind of guy: a Back-of-the-room, Behind-the-scenes Bookworm."* However, he often wonders who this guy is when he hears others list his accomplishments.

Todd never imagined he would be on his current path. He currently teaches leadership in the HR Master's program at NYU. During our conversation, he mentioned that a common topic with HR professionals is having a career path when no one path exists. For most people, their career is *"less like a path, and more like a roller coaster with ups and downs, twists and turns, exhilarating highs, and terrifying plummets."*

His students often think he laid out his whole career plan in advance and his journey to where he ended up today was linear and smooth, but that is anything but the case. Todd remembers being laid off several times and even fired a couple of times, realizing that things he thought he would love he ended up hating and falling in love with jobs he was hesitant to take that changed his life.

In his TEDx Talk, *The Power of Visual Thinking*, Todd reflects on his childhood dream of working in television. He recalls his obsession with TV, recounting his dream of someday being Superman, though willing to settle for Batman as a backup. Realizing years later that those jobs were already taken, he eventually settled for more ordinary roles in the television industry.

He realizes now that as an executive coach and university professor, he embodies and exhibits some of the same characteristics of his childhood superheroes. One of his clients stated, *"In some ways, you are Superman and Batman or aspects of them, but instead of having X-ray vision as Superman does, you have the power of visual thinking. As Batman had his utility belt, you have all these tools, tips, and techniques in your leadership coaching toolkit. What do Superman and Batman do? They rescue people. They are superheroes."*

As Todd points out, what we all need to do is recognize our own superpowers. We also have our kryptonite, the things that we are not good at or are scared of. We can recognize and overcome these things by saying, *"It's okay; we all have flaws. So, how can we counter those things? How can we try to avoid the kryptonite and leverage our superpowers?"*

During his early teen years, Todd realized that it was time to focus on his backup plan of someday working in TV, and based on his personality and the three B's, he was determined to find a back-of-the-room type job. During this time, TV program development caught his eye, and even though he didn't know if he wanted or could be a writer or a producer, he began taking the steps that led in that direction. He majored in English literature in college and admits he stuck with English courses in college because he knew he could do well, but regrets that he didn't take other courses like business. He felt he had to choose between getting a high GPA and learning and exposing himself to new opportunities. Because of what he has learned from this experience, he coaches his students to make the right choice for themselves by asking them, *"When was the last time someone asked you, 'What was your GPA? Or How did you do on your SAT?'"*

Todd spoke about how when we are younger, we don't always know the difference between what we think is important and what is actually important later in life. So it's important to remember to *"Enjoy the little things because someday you will look back and realize those were the big things."* Such a beautiful insight and something we all need to be reminded of occasionally.

Todd's first job after college was as a media buyer. He believed advertising was an excellent first step toward his end goal of working in TV. However, he found himself calculating numbers, commuting two hours per day to a job he didn't love for very little pay, and feeling like this wasn't something he could do forever.

With overtime, I got it up to $15,000, but I was commuting two hours each way from my house. I said, "I can't do this for the rest of my life." I was stuck. I wanted to do something creative. As an introvert, I wasn't the type to raise my hand or speak up and speak out, so I did my job. I applied for a few internal jobs, but they said, "You're a media guy. What do you know about creativity?"

After working as a media buyer for a year and trying to obtain a different position, Todd took his one-week vacation to visit his college roommate in LA. As soon as he arrived, he knew he, too, wanted to be in sunny Hollywood.

Todd began working part-time and temporary jobs to make some money and get by. He recalls getting hired as a bouncer and adapting to the role, much as Superman and Batman did to their identities as heroes. He credits his job as a bouncer for his increase in confidence, and with that increase in confidence, introverted Todd began to put himself out there more.

After a literal punch to the face, Todd found himself looking for different employment. He had a series of jobs, including working for Michael Nesmith from the Monkees, interning for Aaron Spelling, and putting scripts together for Dynasty before working at Columbia Pictures in television and casting. But, little did Todd know, his first big shot was just around the corner.

I was temping for one week in the PR Department, and they needed someone to edit the press release. Unfortunately, all the PR people were at lunch or a meeting. The head of the PR department was annoyed at me. She was yelling and asking me where everyone was. I told her I was answering phones and filing and didn't know where anyone was. She needed a press release edited, proofread and sent out by 2 pm. I asked her if she wanted me to take a shot at it. She said, 'What do you know? You're just a temp.'

I was Todd, the temp. I was sitting there with nothing to do, so I put it on my typewriter and wrote a revision. When the PR guys returned, I said, 'Here's the original. Here's the revision.' I didn't say I did it. The guy looked at it and said, 'This is amazing. This is great. Send it out.' Here I was, a hidden talent. She didn't care that I had a Bachelor's in English and a Master's in Communication. I was labeled as the temp. We never know what our hidden talents are. I had no risk, and there was no downside to my doing it, but I proved to myself that I could do more than what I was doing.

Todd remembers feeling like he was a hidden talent, masked behind the temp title – a bit like Clark Kent. But, of course, we never quite know what our hidden talents are, and this opportunity gave Todd the confidence to recognize he was capable of more than what he was doing.

In Todd's book, he talks about the three V's: visibility, voice, and value, which is all about being seen, heard, and making a contribution. He often tells his students, *"You need to raise your hand; people are not mind-readers."* It's great to be chosen from the crowd, but people with hidden talents – especially introverts, who tend not to toot their horns – are often overlooked. You must be willing to put yourself out there to avoid missing out on opportunities. Todd always reminds his students and coaching clients, *"While we like to think that our work speaks for itself, the reality is that we must speak for our work."*

The Chinese philosopher Lao Tzu said, "When the best leader's work is done, the people say, 'We did it all by ourselves.'" That is the power of an invisible, quiet leader who leads from behind. They step up to take accountability when things fail but give other people credit when things succeed and use inclusive language like, "I am responsible, but we all did this together." I don't know if you ever saw Derek Sivers' video, *First Follower*, where one guy is dancing, but it's the second guy who gets up to dance that starts the movement. You don't always have to go first. Going second or even third, you're still motivating and leading the people who come after you.

Interestingly enough, shortly after his temp nightmare, Todd was hired as a project manager for a theme park company. He was sent to China to oversee a project right off the bat. He remembers being terrified and looking for reasons to get out of the project. Then he found himself leading in a completely different way. His team overcame language barriers by using visuals to communicate.

His experience in China was one of the most exciting, gratifying, and transformative experiences of his career and life. Not only did he have to step up and lead in a foreign land, far from home, where he did not speak the language, but he quickly realized that he could overcome the language barrier and build collaboration by communicating visually. He did not know it then, but this ended up being the origin of his *VisuaLeadership* methodology, TEDx talk, and book.

One of the recurring themes throughout Todd's career is that he worked for a disproportionate number of horrible managers. But while having a toxic boss is one of the most unpleasant and stressful experiences imaginable, the lessons learned were invaluable. And it has given Todd a wealth of stories to tell.

"When I was given my first management job, I had no clue what I was doing. I figured people learned how to manage by watching how they are managed. I don't think I had experienced true leadership at that point. It was literally, 'Now I get to tell people what to do and how to do it right.' I got to put 'Manager' on my business card. Maybe there's a raise that goes along

with it. I eventually learned that leadership is not all about you, but about the people you lead."

In life, setbacks and failures are inevitable, but how we handle them shapes who we become. Todd Cherches is no stranger to these challenges. He has been laid off and fired multiple times, experienced career shifts, and struggled to find his footing in the working world. However, Todd has always approached these setbacks with a growth mindset, using each experience to learn and improve. I love that from each experience, he not only gleans wisdom, but collects it and generously shares it with others. Definitely a superhero characteristic, if you ask me.

Michael O'Brien: Preventing Bad Moments From Turning Into Bad Days

I was thrilled when Michael O'Brien agreed to be on *The Virtual Campfire Podcast*. I resonated with his messages on social media. His mantra, "Pause, Breathe, Reflect," stood out, and I had to learn more about who was behind this message. I discovered a remarkable person who had a powerful story to share.

Michael founded Peloton Executive Coaching and serves on the Healthcare Businesswomen's Association global board. He is also a speaker, a cyclist, and the author of the book *Shift: Creating Better Tomorrows; Winning at Work and in Life*.

Michael's story starts in Rochester, New York, where he grew up with his mom, a nurse, and his dad, who was a salesman. We all have moments in time that stand out to us, and for Michael, the day the training wheels came off his bike is one of those. He remembers having the feeling in that moment, "Now, I can go anywhere."

"For me, the bike could take me far away even though, at that moment, when you were 4 or 5, down the block seemed far away. It was the first moment I felt I had independence and could explore. I fell in love with the bicycle, and that love affair continued through middle school."

Michael's thirst for freedom expanded as a young adult. He was the first in his family to go to university, and of course, like most parents, they preferred he stay close to home. Michael had never traveled far and spent his first year at a university in Rochester commuting to a four-year institution. But, after the first year, he knew he needed to get away.

Eventually, Michael went to school in Virginia, leading him to DC and his first job selling copiers after college. For anyone who has worked in commission sales, you know that sometimes you make great money and other times you don't. Unfortunately, Michael was spending money like he was printing it and found himself with a mountain of credit card debt which was a great lesson in financial responsibility.

In the late 1980s and early 1990s, pharmaceutical sales were growing rapidly. The attraction of talking to doctors about medicine made Michael feel like he could do well in that industry. He landed a pharmaceutical sales job, earning $30 K a year, a healthy bonus, and a company car. He also met his wife and felt like he had it all and was living the dream.

Fast forward to 2001, Michael's last bad day. He was in New Mexico for a company meeting. On the outside, things looked great! Michael had a great gig as a marketing director and made more money than he ever thought possible. He provided a great life for his family and had upgraded from staying in drive-up motels as a kid to fancy hotels. But, on the inside, Michael was riddled with stress. He was chasing happiness instead of actually being happy.

Instead of processing stress, Michael packed it inside and worked it out on the road as an avid cycler. Interested in getting back into racing after the birth of his second daughter, Michael hit the road on July 11, 2001, only to be hit head-on by a Ford Explorer going 40 miles per hour. To this day, he can still remember the details of his accident.

"I was going about 20-ish, then it's everything you learned in high school physics. It makes for a powerful, energetic collision when something's going 20 miles per hour and collides with something going 40. I remember everything about that morning. The sound of me hitting his grill, the sound of me going into the windshield. I still remember vividly the sound of the screech of his brakes, and I got knocked unconscious.

I regained consciousness. When I did, I asked a question that only another cyclist could appreciate. I asked them, 'How's my bike?' I was in the worst pain of my life, and I am cracking a joke because that was how I dealt with challenging moments. I would use humor to diffuse it because I was uncomfortable with difficult situations, and they said, 'Your bike's fine.' A total lie. The bike was destroyed.

They said, 'Try to focus on yourself and breathe.' I knew by their reaction that my life was in question. When they put me on the medevac, I tried to convince them that wasn't the wise thing to do because I was scared of flying back then. I'd never been on a helicopter. We had to fly to Albuquerque, a nineteen-minute flight. It would have been a 45 or 55-minute drive, far too long."

When I got on the helicopter, I made a bargain with myself, *"Michael, if you live, you're going to stop chasing happiness and be present."* It was one of those bargains you make when you feel your end is near. I had no idea how to do it.

"The first surgery lasted about 10 or 12 hours. I had 34 units of blood product and I spent the next four days in the ICU. The doctors told my wife, 'Your husband's been in a bad accident. We did the best we could. The next 72 hours are going to be critical. We're not sure how he survived. If he was

ten years older and not in shape, he would have died before he got to the hospital.' All of a sudden, our world got turned upside down."

Since Michael's accident, he has been motivated to share his learning. But, he says, *"You don't need a traumatic moment to wake up. You can avoid your SUV, but you must live with awareness. Unfortunately, I wasn't living life with much awareness."*

Michael believes there were many smaller moments where he could have made subtle shifts in life before the accident and prevented it altogether. However, he remains *"'grateful that I missed those because the accident has shaped me into the person I am. It has given me a different platform to spread this message to help others. Had it not been for my accident, I might not have had this opportunity to connect with anyone else and share this vital message about how we're living our lives. We've all had our moments.*

Life is hard. We've all had struggles, wrinkles, gray hairs, and scar lines. Some are emotional, and some are physical. Let's embrace them. The message of one scar line or multiple scar lines is still the same as how it shapes us into who we are. We're resilient. We've survived 100% of our bad days if you are reading this now. The pause was another flashpoint where I knew I had to get my mind right and healthy to get my body healthy."

From his hospital room, Michael rolled himself in his wheelchair to a quiet place and set his intentions. It was time to slow everything down. Life moves quickly; we have a lot coming at us that we need to react to. We miss so many moments due to chronic stress, but it's time to change from fast to slow.

Michael's mindfulness practice was born from knowing he needed to get quiet. So his mornings now consist of meditation and mindfulness. *"It was also the spark of what is now Pause, Breathe, Reflect, and it is in hitting pause, reconnecting to our breath, we can slow everything down and be more thoughtful. Be more aware of how we're showing up in our career, our lives, and for those around us."*

Through his mindfulness practice, Michael has learned that his scars are his beauty. When he first came out of the hospital, all the skin grafts he had and all the different scars from his face down to his legs – he tried to cover them up. After that, he had to work hard to get his mind and body right. It was an experience of three steps forward, a few steps backward, then a few more steps ahead. Forward motion was the goal.

"One thing I had difficulty grasping was seeing my scars positively. I saw them as ugly and people were staring at them. I imagine people saying, 'What happened to that guy?' There's so much in this society with vanity and how you look. I had a moment sitting on the couch with my youngest daughter. She was around 7 or 8 at the time. She was mindlessly rubbing one of my skin grafts as a kid. I asked, 'Grace, what do you think of the scars?' She said, I think they're cool.' I didn't want to say that I thought

they were ugly and tried to hide them from everyone else. It was enough of a shift to start appreciating them more and eventually' loving them more. Buying into that whole kintsugi spirit that our scars show this wonderful story of our resilience and beauty."

The concept of Kintsugi is a traditional Japanese art of repairing broken pottery or ceramics with gold or other precious metals. The word "kintsugi" literally means "golden joinery" or "golden repair," and the technique involves mending broken pottery with a lacquer mixed with gold or silver powder. The philosophy behind kintsugi is that breakage and repair are part of the history of an object, and rather than hiding or disguising damage, the broken pieces should be reassembled to highlight the cracks and imperfections. Furthermore, the gold or silver used in the repair process symbolizes beauty and value. Michael took his connection to this concept to another level by launching a podcast called *'The Kintsugi Podcast'* which I had the honor of joining him on.

Michael has many powerful messages, but the biggest takeaway from our conversation is this: *"Scars are also beautiful, whether emotional or physical. I have both from all my different flashpoints, as I am sure you do. Those scars tell this wonderful story about who we are. If we can embrace that and realize that we're all perfectly imperfect, we may give up the chase of perfection. Instead, we realize that we're just going to try to show up and be the best human being we can be."*

Michael O'Brien's story is a testament to the power of failing forward and navigating setbacks. He learned to embrace his scars, seeing them as beautiful reminders of resilience and strength. Michael's accident was a turning point that led him to re-evaluate his life and start living with more awareness. His "Pause, Breathe, Reflect" mantra reminds us to slow down, be present, and make subtle shifts in life before we hit a traumatic moment. We are all perfectly imperfect, and our scars tell a remarkable story about who we are. If we can embrace them, we can give up the chase of perfection and show up as the best human beings we can be.

The Lessons

It's not about how many times you fall, but the number of times you get back up. It's about pushing past your mistakes and reaching the other end with a better perspective. Your biggest mistakes can lead to your biggest successes. Failing forward is an art form; much like all other arts, it requires practice.

Laura Gassner Otting's extensive experience and dedication to helping others navigate their personal and professional lives has led her to the critical concept of consonance, or alignment between one's values and actions. Through her own journey, she has learned the importance of embracing discomfort, recognizing that failure is not fatal, and focusing on the lessons that emerge from setbacks.

Despite numerous setbacks, Todd Cherches consistently demonstrated resilience and a growth mindset. He leveraged his unique abilities and adapted to various roles, eventually becoming an award-winning leadership professor and author. By recognizing and utilizing our own superpowers while overcoming our weaknesses, we can turn adversity into opportunity and transform ourselves into the leaders we aspire to be.

Michael O'Brien embraced his emotional and physical scars and transformed his outlook on life, recognizing the beauty and resilience they represent. A life-threatening accident showed him the power that comes with living intentionally and the importance of processing emotion. Mindfulness is a powerful tool to apply to the idea of failing forward. We talked earlier about taking measured risks and moving forward. Being mindful of our thoughts, our actions, and our reactions means that we can find our own path with more ease and awareness. It may not take running headlong into a truck to alter our path; we can create our paths by learning where we have been and who we were and thinking about where we want to go. We can let go of the fear of failing forward because that means that we get to grow, explore, and further refine ourselves to successfully create the lives we want to lead.

Questions

As we wrap up Lesson 4, let's circle back to the three C's of grounded leadership: curiosity, compassion, and connection, with some questions for you to ponder and journal.

- How can you reframe your mindset to focus on the lesson when challenged in the future?
- What is the most important lesson you have learned from failing at something?
- What things didn't work out the way you wanted, but something different happened that worked out better than you had imagined?
- As a leader, how do you communicate success and failure to the people you work with?

End Notes

"The best way to find yourself is to lose yourself in the service of others." (Mahatma Gandhi)

The Chinese philosopher Lao Tzu said, "When the best leader's work is done, the people say, 'We did it all by ourselves.'" (Lao Tzu)

"First Follower: Leadership Lessons from Dancing Guy." YouTube, February 11, 2010, https://www.youtube.com/watch?v=fW8amMCVAJQ. Accessed June 19, 2023.

The Startup of You – Reid Hoffman and Ben Casnocha

Limitless – Laura Gassner Otting

Wonderhell – Laura Gassner Otting

VisuaLeadership – Todd Cherches

Shift – Michael O'Brien

Disrupt Your Thinking

Often, we find ourselves stuck in patterns where everything seems to be happening on autopilot. Some of these patterns make us more productive, but at some point, we need to stop and see if they are still serving us. Sometimes we must disrupt our patterns to grow into the person we are meant to be. Tapping into disruptive thinking is like a wake-up call to living with intention, but it doesn't always feel like it in the moment.

Personal disruption is a concept that has gained significant attention in recent years, thanks in part to the work of Whitney Johnson, a leading expert on the subject. In her book *Disrupt Yourself,* Johnson explores the idea that individuals can proactively create change in their lives by embracing a mindset of disruptive thinking. At its core, disruption involves taking risks and challenging the status quo. It's about pushing yourself outside of your comfort zone, identifying your strengths and weaknesses, and seeking out new opportunities for growth and development. This mindset can be applied to any area of life, from personal relationships to career goals.

Whitney's approach to personal disruption is rooted in the theory of disruptive innovation, which she studied while working as an analyst on Wall Street. She applies the principles of disruptive innovation to individuals, arguing that we can all benefit from disrupting our own lives in the same way that businesses can benefit from disrupting their industries.

One key aspect of personal disruption is "playing to our strengths." Whitney argues that you can find new opportunities for growth and success by identifying your unique skills and abilities. This means being willing to take on new challenges and tasks, even if they're outside your current area of expertise.

Another aspect of personal disruption is the willingness to embrace failure. We talked a lot about failure in the last chapter, and it is also an essential part of disruptive thinking. It is important to view failure as an opportunity for growth rather than a setback. We can become more resilient and adaptable by taking risks and learning from our mistakes.

DOI: 10.4324/9781003364818-6

So whether you are looking to advance your career, build stronger personal relationships, or become a better version of yourself, the principles of personal disruption can help you achieve your goals.

We must remember that our thoughts are incredibly powerful. They shape our perceptions, feelings, and behaviors. And sometimes, our thoughts can hold us back, causing us to experience anxiety, self-doubt, and other negative emotions. To break free from these limiting thoughts, we need to disrupt them, and that process starts with awareness. So often, our thoughts operate on autopilot, running in the background of our minds without us even noticing. But we can identify patterns and triggers by paying attention to and tuning into our thoughts.

For example, imagine you have a fear of public speaking. Whenever you have to give a presentation or speak in front of a group, you feel a sense of dread and anxiety. However, if you take a moment to reflect on your thoughts in those moments, you might notice that you're thinking things like "I'm going to mess up," "I'm not good enough," or "Everyone is going to judge me." Once you've identified these thoughts, the next step is to disrupt them. This means challenging them and questioning whether they're really true. For example, if you think, "I'm not good enough," ask yourself, "Is that true? Have I ever given a presentation that went well? What evidence do I have to support that thought?" By disrupting these negative thoughts, you can reframe them in a more positive and realistic light. This can help to reduce anxiety and build confidence.

Disrupting our thoughts starts with awareness. It takes practice, but we can break free from limiting beliefs by paying attention to and questioning our thoughts to build a more positive and empowering mindset.

Many of us find ourselves being reactive rather than proactive. We go through our days reacting to whatever is happening, putting out fires, stopping impending disasters, and tackling what's showing up – it begins to feel like a grind. During these moments, we are simply getting through our days, exhausted and feeling like we're not gaining traction or making forward progress. This is because reactivity stifles our ability to be creative. It takes a mindset shift to become proactive and to start creating our world rather than just reacting to it. Disrupting our thinking becomes imperative. When we repeatedly think the same thoughts and stay stuck in the same mindset, we will be taken for a ride rather than creating the path.

Reactivity is a form of survival mode. Reactivity comes from our primal brain, which is a narrower thinking pattern. It is meant to be focused on survival's sake but isn't as helpful today when there are no large predators to fight. Survival mode prevents us from seeing all of the possibilities around us.

One way to disrupt is by slowing down and observing more of what is happening around us. Many of us learned that if a problem arises, we need to take action swiftly, but what happens is that we often prevent ourselves from taking the time to identify all of the creative solutions that are available to us.

Now that we have touched on the concept of disruptive thinking, it is time to explore some inspiring examples so you can see the power of this mindset in driving personal and professional growth. The people in the following stories have embraced disruption and used it to serve others in their own unique ways. These individuals embody the transformative potential of disruptive thinking by challenging the status quo, taking risks, and continually seeking self-improvement.

Kelly Wendorf: Connecting to Self and Nature to Find Your Way

I met Kelly Wendorf when I visited her breathtaking Thunderbird Ridge ranch in Santa Fe, New Mexico. It was an experience that I continue to cherish to this day. Spending time with Kelly and her herd of horses was a powerful and spiritual experience. Her presence was warm and inviting, but I immediately felt a world of insights waiting to be uncovered from her past.

Kelly is the founding partner of EQUUS, a leadership development organization operating at the Thunderbird Ridge ranch. In addition, she is a Master Certified Coach and the author of *Flying Lead Change: 56 Million Years of Wisdom for Leading and Living*. Kelly's work sits at the nexus of neuroscience, ancient wisdom, systems theory, and nature-based intelligence.

She has lived and worked around the world, studying with many spiritual and Indigenous leaders in India, Africa, Indonesia, and Australia. Immersion in multicultural perspectives honed her passion for creating a new narrative in the human condition, empowering organizations, and their leaders to wield meaningful change through servant leadership and innovative business development.

When Kelly and I began our conversation, she shared a flashpoint that happened early in her life and ultimately shaped her worldview for the rest of her life.

"My father is an archeologist. He was well-known in his field, and when I was a small child, we traveled around the world a lot. When I was seven, he took us to Ethiopia, and we spent several weeks there. It was the 1970s, and my brother and I, two tiny blonde white children in Ethiopia's bush, were a political target.

My father hired an Oromo warrior, the Indigenous people of Ethiopia, to take care of us while he was in the field doing his work. This warrior's job was to be alongside my brother and me in the desert to protect us from baboons and kidnappings. This man became my friend, even though we did not speak the same language. We were not from the same culture, and I am sure he was at least 20 to 30 years older than me.

We shared a silent language. He took good care of me, but there was something underneath the words and everything that was between the two of us. To have this companionship collided with how I had been conditioned as a child in America around what it means to be human, including race, class, and all these things that we take on when we're socialized as children. This man was not any of the things that I had known or understood before. It broke a spell of what it means to be human because he lived as a free man in many ways, and our connection was so outside of societal norms.

When it was time for us to leave after these weeks, I waited for him to see us off. He was sitting alone in a chair, and it was dark because it was early morning. I jumped up on his lap because I could tell he was very sad, but I didn't notice until a few moments later that he was weeping. We held each other, and it was my first time seeing a man cry. This experience broke open my heart and mind.

That is what happened to me in the embrace of this beautiful man who loved me so completely, even though we were not family and did not know each other in a traditional sense. So when I left Ethiopia, I felt different than the other children. I thought I had seen goodness in humanity that wasn't available in the protected layers of modern society.

From that point forward, it set me on a trajectory to be an outsider, the weird kid, much more comfortable in nature, with traditional people wherever I could find them, and with animals and places where that kind of communion is possible. I couldn't find it in school, college, or work. There was some incongruence between how we were being socialized as human beings and this deep, heartful, free capacity to love and care for one another that I had experienced.

That was a real pivotal flashpoint, and it led me to unconventional places to seek my answers. I spent many years in India studying with spiritual teachers. As a mother, I had both of my children at home. I was doing that differently, looking at the science behind raising children, birthing children, and deciding to color outside the lines because I wanted to align with ancient wisdom and nature's way.

I met an influential teacher named Uncle Bob Randall. He is the listed custodial elder of Uluru, which is Ayers Rock in Australia. He enlisted me to transcribe some of his teachings to ensure they would live on for future generations. We spent many days together, weeks, and months over a long stretch of time, where he downloaded lots of information from their 60,000-year-old culture around the right relationship to ourselves, the earth, and each other.

Their people are oral tradition based. So it was quite an opportunity to record his words, transcribe them and go back to him and say, 'What did you mean when you said this? How does this connect with this?' So it was a deep dive into these ancient teachings, which resonated with my experience in Ethiopia when I was seven.

This experience has had a significant influence on my work as a coach. As a lifelong horsewoman, it has also impacted how I work with my horses. It is about deconstructing oppressive mindsets, ideologies, and structures that we all live inside – because we are modern people who have been commercialized – and deconstructing those to find our authentic way of living in the world. Who are we outside of who we have been trained to be, who we have been taught we should be, and who we think we need to be for others? Who is that authentic, unique, gifted, and bright light of a human inside of us? My real interest is deconstructing those things for people so that they can shine forward."

Her father may not have had any idea of the far-reaching effects his journey would ultimately elicit, yet it still provided an incredible learning opportunity. Despite being consumed by work, her dad opened the door to invaluable lessons that continue to inform and influence her life today.

"We should talk about leading from behind. What my father did, whether he realized it or not, was create the conditions for me to find my way. It wasn't deliberate, but so be it. The point is that he created the conditions for me to take the lessons forward.

You can create the right conditions, but each person has to choose what to make of it. Then, they will either take the opportunity or not. A lot of people ask, "What's leading from behind?" It is a way of emotionally, psychically, and spiritually positioning yourself as a leader so that it pushes others out to the fore so that they can shine.

Many people don't think they are leaders because they imagine leading is out front and somehow being in the spotlight. But, on the contrary, the most powerful leadership is when you, as a leader, have enabled those you serve to be emboldened and be all they can be to the point where they don't even know you are doing anything."

Kelly talks about how she navigated the world through a different lens and realized her gift was learning that she wouldn't be able to live like everyone else. In some ways, that can be a burden. But it also allowed her to disrupt societal patterns for herself and others. However, her process of transformation has been a challenging one.

"If you are in the transformation business, you will get many teachings on navigating change. You start to wonder when it will stop. When do we stop transforming? The answer is never. Life was most challenging when I veered off the path and started living outside my integrity.

I believe there's so much anxiety in the world today because we are not in alignment. We live into what we think we need to be and feel anxious. We take medications for anxiety. But often, I believe that our fear is telling us something. We need to stop putting ourselves in boxes. We need to live more authentically, more intentionally.

Our bodies are excellent barometers for when we are off course. For example, when I feel tight, diminished, and anxious, somewhere, I am entertaining something too constricting for me. So I might need to create some expansion by revisiting my beliefs or habits and see if there is a pattern that I need to change to get back on track."

I asked Kelly about her love of horses and what led her to start EQUUS. And she shared some great insights about her journey.

"When I was around seven, I met my first horse. My godmother brought him to our front yard in the middle of the city. I will never forget it; for the rest of my life, I was utterly intoxicated by this creature. They have been, and continue to be, my most strict and committed teachers.

The only place I wanted to be was bareback on my horse, running around the countryside, and that's where I spent my childhood, on the back of a horse. Then, in my 20s, I started riding school.

I was a professional dressage rider and trainer and was in that equestrian world entirely, another world full of concepts and limiting structures. There was a point where I felt in my bones the suffering that happens to horses in that world. We say we love them, but there's still a tool to get over that fence, get that ribbon, and push that cow. There are some exceptional equestrians out there, but very few treat the horse as a sentient being equal to ourselves. I couldn't live with that; I didn't know how to reconcile with the cost to these incredible creatures.

I threw the whole thing away. That's when I went to India and vowed never to go near the equestrian world again, but the horses wouldn't leave me alone. So I immigrated to Australia as a single mother of two young children. I had to put food on the table, so I founded a magazine called Kindred. Kindred was a very ambitious project. The magazine's premise was asking this one question: How do we raise a just and sustainable society?

That's a very ambitious question. We pulled articles from lots of academic places and brought an evidence-based exploration into how we raise a just and sustainable society. We looked at parenthood, birthing practices, healthcare, and local farming. That is where I learned so much about neuroscience. And I decided that I wanted to bring all this together. So we have the Indigenous piece, which started when I was seven, with the horse piece that began to weave in, and then we had the Kindred experience.

I put myself at the feet of many neuroscientists looking at how our brains are shaped, how they're influenced, and how they change and grow. To me, that was like, "Wow." It is exciting that 66% of our brain can change, and 33% we're stuck with. So I geeked out on neuroscience, and I still do.

I started to learn the art of horse whispering while I was in Australia, which was a much more nuanced and equitable relationship with horses. Once

I started listening to the horses rather than talking to them about everything they should do for me, something magical happened.

All these doors started opening to me about the horses' capacity to liberate us. They can allow us to experience wisdom, courage, love, openness, a sense of adventure, and an understanding of boundaries. I discovered that they have the power to help us find connection, peace, and joy.

I immigrated back to the States, donated the magazine to a nonprofit, returned to Santa Fe, and started a new chapter of my life. So what do I do with these teachings from my life journey? Well, I got trained as a coach and integrated them into one bundle, with horses and the wisdom of nature as a foundation.

Neuroscience and coaching bring together an approach to coaching that is truly transformative. We have this herd of six horses and a donkey. People who come to the ranch to work with the horses have a transformational experience.

The horse is a grounding creature. The bottom of their feet has a spongy, squishy part that touches the Earth, and from that point, a central arterial system connects to the heart. So the horse is feeling the Earth's electro-magnetic pulse through their heart. They are an active conduit to the Earth. When we interact with horses, they positively influence our nervous system. In a way, they are a tuning fork, and your body tunes itself when you are around them."

I found this so interesting and inspiring, and I love how it challenges common thinking of horses as a means to an end rather than a relationship that connects you to the Earth itself. So the next thing I asked Kelly was if she had any parting words of advice before I let her go, and this is what she shared:

"Don't believe anything you have learned about who you should be. At first, it may feel real, but if you look at it closely, you'll see it's a construct. Secondly, everyone on this planet is destined to serve in some way. So what is your way of contributing? Lastly, as the Indigenous people knew, and we have lost our way a bit, you can only navigate this world effectively with access to that natural world."

Kelly's insight on tapping into the natural world and challenging societal and personal beliefs was vital to disrupting her thinking. She chose time and time again to dig deeper, stay curious, ask hard questions, and connect with traditional and ancient wisdom in her search for her place on this Earth.

In the captivating story of Kelly Wendorf, we witness the power of a young girl's life-altering experience in Ethiopia that shaped her worldview and set her on a path of self-discovery and transformation. Throughout her life, Kelly has sought the wisdom of ancient cultures, the teachings of nature, and the insights of neuroscience to develop her unique approach to coaching, leadership, and personal growth. By weaving together these various threads of knowledge, Kelly has created a tapestry that challenges societal norms and encourages a more authentic, intentional way of living. Through her work at EQUUS and her love for horses, she has found a way to foster deep connections between people, animals, and the Earth itself. Kelly's story is a testament to the power of embracing our unique gifts, questioning the constructs we have learned, and seeking guidance from the wisdom of nature and the world around us.

Whitney Johnson: Growth Is Our Default Setting

Disruption is a part of growth and transformation. We disrupt our daily routine to create opportunities to change for the better. Whitney Johnson is one of the prominent names in personal growth and disruption; for a good reason, she has written numerous books on the subject, including *Dare, Dream, Do, Disrupt Yourself, Build an A-Team*, and *Smart Growth*. Her books have been a blueprint for creating growth paths for people and their journeys. Whitney is also the founder and CEO of the leadership development company Disruption Advisors and one of the top 50 business thinkers in the world, according to *Thinkers50*. And I can't leave out that she hosts the incredible *Disrupt Yourself Podcast*. I had the pleasure of working with her as a Smart Growth Advisor when Whitney launched the company, and it has been fantastic to see the impact we have had on so many organizations along the way.

In Whitney's TEDx Talk, Disrupt Yourself, she shares how she went from a secretary to the CEO of her own company. Whitney talks about living in New York with her husband while he was working on his doctorate and deciding that she would work on Wall Street. When she considered her limitations, she noted that she was a female, a music major, hadn't gone to an Ivy League school, and had no experience. Whitney found herself working as an administrative assistant. At some point, she wondered what her life would look like if she went from making X to making 10X, and an idea formed. She went to night school and began working in the finance world, and after ten years in the industry, climbing the ladder along the way, she disrupted herself yet again.

Companies are constantly disrupting, whether it is themselves, other companies, or their industry. When the environment changes, they need to pivot or shift direction. People can do that for themselves as well, and Whitney believes that by disrupting your vision of yourself, you can harness tremendous capacity for innovation and success. I won't go into her entire talk, but I highly recommend checking it out. In our conversation, she shared how she learned to apply the term "disrupt" to what she was doing and how learning to disrupt her thinking became a catalyst for her growth.

She was working on Wall Street, where she excelled at building financial models and had an eagle eye for identifying momentum in a stock. She co-founded the Disruptive Innovation Fund with Clayton Christensen, who many people know as the writer of a book called *The Innovator's Dilemma*, in which he coined the term "Disruptive Innovation."

"One of the things that I discovered while I was still working on Wall Street was that I was more interested in people and the momentum of people than I was in the momentum of stocks. So instead of thinking about what stocks will go up, I thought of people as if they were stocks, 'How do I help this person build momentum?' So when I read Innovator's Dilemma and thought about disruption, I thought, 'You can apply this to people too. People can disrupt themselves.'

I started applying disruption concepts and theories to people, using the idea of an S curve to describe how we learn and grow. First, I wrote articles in the Harvard Business Review about my thoughts, and eventually, those ideas evolved into Disrupt Yourself.

Sometimes, the things we are called to do, we run away from them. We must be aware of the truth-tellers who tell us, 'That's your gift. You need to use that gift. You are a cheerleader at heart. You care about the momentum of people. Now figure out what that will look like and how you will do that.' I realized that I didn't want to do stocks. I wanted to talk about people and how people grow."

Whitney had to disrupt herself to get into disrupting how people grow. That moment is remarkable and indeed life-changing. She applied the idea of disrupting markets to see an opportunity to bring this concept into her own life and other people's lives.

She developed her S curve of learning model to explain the process by which we grow, which she discusses in greater detail in her books. The S curve of learning is a visual model for us to view what growth looks and feels like. The model is based on the diffusion curve popularized by E. M. Rogers in the 60s to determine how quickly groups of people change.

Every time you start something new, you begin at the *Launch Point*, which is the base of the "S." At this point, you may feel discouraged or impatient. Even though growth is happening, it's not readily apparent.

The second phase of the S curve of learning is where you hit that steep back of the curve, which she refers to as the *Sweet Spot*. Now you're beginning to understand more, make predictions, and receive positive results. In this phase, you feel competent and confident. You're feeling all the effects of dopamine, as you are at a place where it's still hard, but not too hard and easier, but not too easy. You may feel exhilarated, and the growth is fast.

The third part of the curve is called *Mastery*, and this is the place where you have figured everything out. However, you can become bored since you no longer get the feel-good effects of learning. Growth slows again because you're learning less, and it's less exciting.

So overall, the curve shows us that the learning and growth experience is slow, then fast, then slow again. Understanding this model can help you increase your capacity to grow. Knowing where you fall in this curve at any given time can help motivate you to keep going and give you a sense of normalcy in your feelings at any given point.

"The S curve of learning provides us with a map, giving us a simple visual of what growth looks like. Alexander Osterwalder once told me, 'When you write a book, you should be able to write your book in pictures. You should have a picture forChapters 1, 2, 3, etc.' And this model really connects with that idea.

We are in this era right now where we all want to grow. We're coming out of the pandemic, post-traumatic growth. You come through this period of severe stress, which I do not like to refer to as the Great Resignation. I believe it is the Great Aspiration. We are aspiring to more. This book gives you a map of what growth looks like. You know where you are, and you know what's next. You know whether you're at the launch point of the curve, the sweet spot of the curve, and mastery along the curve.

All those places along the curve have specific things you want or need to do; whether it is support, focus, or a challenge, the map can help you navigate the path. It is like the lexicon you use in your work, Tony, Climbing the Right Mountain, where you need to check in to see where you are on the mountain and where you are going. Then, once you orient yourself, you can move up the mountain more intentionally."

Her books have gone on to be a great success, and she's even expanded her S curve disruption model to include teams in her new book *Smart Growth*.

"I start the book by saying, 'Growth is our default setting.' I have always wanted to grow. I've always wanted to make progress. It's this hunger that I have, and I believe that everybody does. We all want to make progress. We all want to learn. So if I think about being on Wall Street, disrupting myself, and moving on from investing to thought leadership and building Disruption Advisors – all of those moments were about my desire to grow."

One of my favorite moments from our interview that perfectly illustrated the patience with growth was when she read me the 60-year-old children's book *The Carrot Seed*:

"A little boy planted a carrot seed. His mother said, 'I'm afraid it won't come up.'

His father said, 'I'm afraid it won't come up.' His big brother said, 'It won't come up.' So every day, the little boy pulled up the weeds around the seed and sprinkled the ground with water, but nothing came up.

Everyone kept saying it wouldn't come up, but he still pulled up the weeds around it every day and sprinkled the ground with water.

Then one day, the carrot came up just as a little boy had known it would."

Whitney Johnson's inspiring story and her work in the field of personal growth and disruption demonstrate that growth is not a linear process. We must disrupt our thinking, shift our focus, and be patient while learning something new. On your own journey of growth and transformation, remember the S curve of learning and think about what stage you might be going through. With this understanding, we can better navigate our paths, embrace change, and propel ourselves forward. Like the little boy in *The Carrot Seed* story, our determination, patience, and unwavering belief in ourselves will ultimately lead us to growth and success. So, dare to disrupt yourself and witness the incredible power of self-disruption in shaping your future.

The Lessons

In the journey of personal and professional growth, disruptive thinking plays a significant role. Disrupting our thinking patterns and embracing change can be daunting, but the rewards are immeasurable. Throughout history, there have been many people who have adopted disruptive thinking and achieved tremendous success. As we have seen, these exceptional leaders demonstrated some beautiful examples of how we can disrupt ourselves and create a meaningful impact.

Kelly Wendorf showed us how connecting to ourselves and nature can be a catalyst for shifting our mindsets and how we navigate the world. Honoring yourself and your place in this world can give you insights into your path that you might otherwise miss. Kelly embraced being an outsider, she felt like an outsider after her experience in Ethiopia, but it ultimately gave her the freedom to live and think outside societal norms. Embracing being an outsider can allow you to see things differently and approach challenges with a fresh perspective. Nature-based wisdom can be a powerful source of inspiration and learning. Kelly's love for horses and nature inspired her to learn the art of horse whispering and incorporate it into her coaching practice. Tapping into the natural world can help individuals connect with themselves, their communities, and the world in new and meaningful ways.

Whitney Johnson's work on personal growth and disruption teaches us that embracing change and disrupting our thinking is essential for growth and transformation. Growth is not a linear process, and we will encounter moments of slow progress and setbacks. By disrupting our vision of ourselves and embracing new challenges, we can tap into our capacity for innovation and success. By daring to disrupt ourselves and navigate the

S curve of learning, we can propel ourselves forward on our journeys of growth and transformation.

Questions

As we wrap up Lesson 5, let's circle back to the three C's of grounded leadership: curiosity, compassion, and connection, with some questions for you to ponder and journal.

- Can you identify any patterns, triggers, or negative thinking that you could shift in a positive direction?
- How can you practice slowing down and observing your surroundings to help you be more creative and proactive in your thinking?
- What areas do you feel stuck or stagnant in your life? How might disrupting your current routine help you make progress in these areas?
- How can you make disruption a regular part of your life to continually push yourself to grow and learn?

End Notes

Tedx Talks "TEDxEmbarcadero – Whitney Johnson – Disrupt Yourself." YouTube, May 4, 2011, https://www.youtube.com/watch?v=FPFMcCgWCdg. *Accessed June 19, 2023.*
    Disrupt Yourself – Whitney Johnson
    Flying Lead Change – Kelly Wendorf
    Dare, Dream, Do – Whitney Johnson
    Build an A-Team – Whitney Johnson
    Smart Growth – Whitney Johnson
    Innovator's Dilemma – Clayton Christensen
    The Carrot Seed – Ruth Krauss

Don't Put Yourself in a Box

Humans are constantly evolving beings with the capacity for growth and change. We all have unique personalities, perspectives, and experiences. However, we often limit ourselves by putting ourselves in a box, defining ourselves by one or two traits, or adhering to certain societal norms. These norms can dictate our expectations, limiting how we express ourselves or even shaping our identity. Even our career paths and education choices can be influenced by societal expectations, leading us to stop exploring and experimenting. This keeps us from growing and limits our potential to achieve our goals and aspirations.

When asked about ourselves, we often begin by sharing the labels we have acquired over the years. I am a father, husband, coach, speaker, etc. You get the idea. We talk about our jobs and our relationships with other people. We usually mention our age, origins, hobbies, athletic endeavors, or musical preferences. The point is no matter how we classify ourselves, we are looking for overlaps to connect with others. However, what would it look like to connect with things that are foreign to you instead of looking for someone with whom you are perfectly aligned?

Sometimes our boxes are preprogrammed paths that lie before us, and we think we must take them and not stray. Maybe we have been told to act a certain way, dress a certain way, follow a specific career path, and retire by a certain age. We do so many things simply because we are "supposed to." But according to whom? Who makes the rules of the life you are going to lead? When it's all said and done, when you reflect on your life, will you be happy that you colored within the lines, or will you regret not stepping off your prescribed path to take new opportunities?

Labeling and categorizing each other is also a part of our human design because it helps us make sense of the world; however, when we try to fit neatly into a defined box, we unfairly judge people. We limit our capacity to see ourselves and others as individuals with unique experiences, thoughts, and feelings. When we focus only on the set of characteristics or

DOI: 10.4324/9781003364818-7

labels that we associate with a particular group rather than connecting with people on a deeper level, we miss the big picture.

We might intuitively know that we are more than our titles, but we need to open ourselves up to see the full spectrum of our capabilities and strengths. It can be overwhelming to realize that you are so much more powerful than you first thought. Yet, once you harness your inner brilliance, you can use it to shape your world. It can start from just one flashpoint that changes how you see everything around you. And this one flashpoint can unlock your true potential.

Have you ever noticed how one thing can change everything? Four thousand years ago, in ancient Mesopotamia, a group of people started experimenting by adding heat to sand, soda, and lime, creating glass for the first time. Today that one thing has allowed us to invent microscopes that see down to the building blocks of life and telescopes, allowing us to see back to the beginning of the universe.

Until 1954, it was considered impossible for a human to run a mile in less than four minutes. And then Roger Bannister instantly changed the entire world by doing it. After that, others immediately began to break the four-minute mile as well. Sometimes all it takes to create massive change is to achieve one thing. One insight. One realization. One move can change the entire game and set a new path for everyone else to follow. Can you recall a time when you made one choice, and from that choice, you watched your life unfold on a new positive path?

If you feel stuck in your work, held back in your business, or limited in your life, I want you to know that an insight is just waiting for you. And what it takes to get that insight and let it grow into a game changer is to keep going. You have to keep putting one step in front of the next, even when it feels daunting.

Let's explore how this lesson relates to the three C's of grounded leadership: curiosity, compassion, and connection.

By seeing each person as unique and complex, we can break down the barriers that separate us, build stronger relationships, and recognize our shared humanity. When we see others as separate from ourselves, it becomes easy to view them as "other" or "different," which can lead to feelings of isolation and distrust. By seeking out connections with others, we can break down these barriers and build a sense of empathy and understanding. To foster connection, we must be willing to step outside our comfort zones and engage with people who may be different from us. This can involve listening to their stories, sharing our own experiences, and finding common ground. Doing so can build a sense of shared humanity and create a more inclusive and compassionate world.

When we approach people with curiosity, we open ourselves up to learning about their unique experiences and perspectives. This not only helps us to understand them better, but it also allows us to see the world in new and different ways. To cultivate curiosity, we must be willing to ask questions and listen without judgment. This involves being open to the possibility that our assumptions and beliefs may be incorrect and being willing to learn from others. By embracing curiosity, we can break down stereotypes and assumptions and create a more inclusive and accepting society.

Compassion is the foundation of any healthy relationship. It involves recognizing the struggles and challenges that others face and responding with empathy and kindness. When we approach others compassionately, we create a safe and supportive environment where people can be themselves and feel valued. To cultivate compassion, we must be willing to put ourselves in others' shoes and see the world from their perspective. This involves listening with an open heart, acknowledging their experiences, and responding with empathy and kindness. By approaching others compassionately, we can break down the walls that separate us and create a more connected and supportive world.

Putting people in boxes can limit our ability to connect with others and see them as individuals. Instead, by cultivating a sense of connection, curiosity, and compassion, we can break down the barriers that separate us and build stronger relationships. This involves stepping outside our comfort zones and embracing new experiences and perspectives.

This chapter will explore the concept of not putting ourselves in a box and how it can be liberating and empowering. These incredible visionaries decided they did not want to settle for conventional results or be defined by others. Instead, they chose to live outside the box, without any constraints, to embrace their full potential.

Ozan Varol: Unconventional Journey to Success

Ozan Varol is definitely someone you cannot put into a box. He is a rocket scientist turned award-winning professor, a best-selling author, and a thought leader. He is one of the world's foremost creativity, innovation, and critical-thinking experts. His work has been featured in the Wall Street Journal, Time, BBC, CNN, Washington Post, and more. His books *Think Like a Rocket Scientist* and *Awaken Your Genius* are brilliant, but I am an even bigger fan of his weekly blog, which is both inspiring and insightful.

As a native of Istanbul, Turkey, he learned English as a second language and moved to the United States at 17 to attend Cornell University and major in astrophysics. Ozan lived in a small apartment in Istanbul when he was four years old. Turkey was a developing country at that time, and there were regular blackouts. Young Ozan was terrified when the power was out, and his dad devised a game to distract and entertain him. One of his favorite toys was his soccer ball, so when the power went out, Ozan's Dad would light a candle and grab his soccer ball. He used the candle and soccer ball to model how the Earth rotated around the sun. It reduced Ozan's fear of the darkness and fascinated him. In addition, it opened his eyes to the world beyond what he could see.

Through today's eyes, Ozan sees these memories as his first lessons in astrophysics, which put him on the path to where he is today. Once his interest was piqued, he began to buy every science book he could afford and regularly lost himself in the worlds created by some of the greats. Little did Ozan know his interest would blossom into majoring in astrophysics and having opportunities like being a part of the Mars Exploration Rovers Project operations team.

Considering that Ozan moved to the United States at only 17 years old and could barely speak English, it's impressive how his journey unfolded.

"My parents instilled in me a sense of autonomy from a very early age. One example that's symbolic of how they raised me is when I was about to enter kindergarten. The way that the system works in Istanbul is you've got 4 or 5 kindergartens within driving distance of your house. You can pick any one you want. My parents researched these schools and visited them. They came home to me and said, 'You are now going to start kindergarten, and you've got three choices. We'll take you to them, and you can pick which one you want. Think through what questions you want to ask. What do you find important?' I was a five-year-old boy, and they gave me so much autonomy. Any one of these three kindergartens would work well for them. Having set up those guard rails and allowing me to walk into these schools, I felt like an adult.

I asked them the questions that I found important, like 'What kind of toys do you have? What kind of books do you have? Do you have science fiction books?' All the things that I found important at that age left a lasting mark. The poem Invictus comes to mind, 'I am the master of my fate. I am the captain of my soul.' That idea was instilled in me by my parents at a very young age. Regardless of the circumstances we were in, economic and otherwise, the possibilities in life are limitless. If you want something, it's up to you to go and get it. That lesson stayed with me to this day."

Like anyone else, Ozan has experienced obstacles on his journey too.

"In my experience, the obstacles tend to be the stories we tell ourselves. That story doesn't necessarily come internally. Instead, it's a story that we were told to believe in by societal conditioning or by conditioning from our parents or education system, which plays a huge role in curbing our autonomy and a sense of believing that smaller dreams are wiser than moonshots. So when you combine those three factors, society, family, and the education system, you end up with limiting beliefs that stay with you for a long time. Identifying those beliefs and knowing how to manage them is important."

When Ozan was accepted to Cornell and spent the last few weeks in Turkey before heading to the United States, he decided to research what the astrophysics department was up to. He learned that one of the professors was in charge of NASA's mission to Mars. While there were no active job listings, Ozan reached out to see if there were any opportunities to work on the project. He distinctly remembers the voice of self-doubt popping into his head as he was about to hit send on the email.

"It was the voice of, 'You're a skinny kid with a funny name from a country halfway around the globe. What could you possibly contribute? There is no job listing. So why are you even sending an email to this important person?' That voice hasn't completely disappeared. It still comes up from time to time.

I asked myself two questions. The first one is, 'What is the worst that can happen? What would I do if that worst thing were to actually happen?' In that case, the worst thing that would happen is he'd never write back to me. He'd ignore it, think I was out of my mind, and that would be that. I would never hear from him again.

I asked myself, 'What is the best that can happen?' The best that can happen is I would land a 'pinch me now' job working on the operations team for this Mars mission. When you put it that way, the choice is so obvious. So I clicked send, and I'm so glad I did because mustering up the courage to send that email triggered the series of events that led to me writing Think Like a Rocket Scientist and publishing that book.

I still use those two questions on a regular basis. Whenever I'm afraid of taking a leap into the unknown, I ask myself, 'What's the worst that can happen?' It's a bit more nuanced than that now, 'What's the worst thing that can happen? How likely is that thing to actually happen?' Usually, our worst-case scenarios are highly unlikely. If that were to happen, what would I do? What's the best that can happen? Our minds are good at generating horrible scenarios. It's very nice, in my view, and essential to counterbalance that with, 'What is the best that can happen?'

To make sure you don't get stuck in that mode, write down your answers. I find that hypothetically thinking about worst-case scenarios can end up making them worse, but something about writing them down has a way of disempowering them. When you see your fears with the masks off, written down, I often find that the feeling of that fear is worse than the thing I fear. Writing them down is an excellent way of dressing down your fears and seeing them with their masks off."

After four years on the Mars Exploration Rovers Project, Ozan switched gears and went to law school. He practiced law for two years and then pivoted again to teaching law. In 2021, Ozan decided that would be his last year teaching and took a leap of faith into writing a book to help others make giant leaps in their lives.

Ozan explained the backcasting strategy he used to successfully reach his goals:

"With forecasting, you're projecting the status quo into the future. All of your problematic assumptions and biases get compounded. With backcasting, you work backward from the desired outcome. In my case, back in 2016, writing a mainstream book for a lay audience was my moonshot, and I worked backward from that. What do you need to be able to publish a book with a major publisher? You need an agent. How do you get an agent? You need a referral from somebody who already knows and has worked with that agent. You need a big platform, ideally, people who are already reading what you're writing. That led to me working back from that desired outcome. It led me to launch a blog in 2016, and a year later, I followed up with a podcast. Those decisions eventually got me an agent and then led to the publication of Think Like a Rocket Scientist.

There's a poem I love from Dawna Markova called I Will Not Die an Unlived Life. This is a stanza that I've memorized, 'I choose to risk my significance so that what comes to me as seed can move on as blossom, and what comes to me as blossom can go on as fruit.' Particularly the line, 'I choose to risk my significance,' whenever I'm afraid of taking a leap now, that line comes to me as echoes from my subconscious, reminding me that I've got nothing to lose."

Ozan is more focused on the process than becoming attached to the outcome. He believes when you can do this, it allows you to see possibilities instead of limitations. He recalled that adopting this mindset was the key that eventually unlocked his success. Focusing on the process instead of the outcome made all the difference.

Like many of us, Ozan sometimes chose the safe option in his life and career. He has learned that *"You look at it one day and realize the safety net is actually a straitjacket because it allows you to only play in this one safe area. It boxes you into an area because you don't have a safety net anywhere else. You're only going to play in this one area. Safety nets are important, but over time, you outgrow them, and even if you don't outgrow them, they have a way of confining you, which is when the safety net turns into a straitjacket.*

So, at that time, you've got to take it off because if you don't, you're going to be confined and boxed in, and you will die an unlived life"

Fast forward to 2020 and the pandemic. Ozan found himself impacted by a roadblock like many other entrepreneurs. He had worked incredibly hard on his book, which was published in the early days of the pandemic.

"I have found that the universe has a way of setting up walls to separate those who want something from those who don't. There's always some roadblock towards the end whenever I have come close to achieving something. It's almost like this test of, 'Do you really want this?' You can go over

that roadblock and figure out a way around it if you want it. If you don't want it, then you can give up.

This happened with the launch of my book. I worked on the book for a long time, and it was published on April 14, 2020, at the height of the pandemic. A month before the book comes out, the whole world shuts down. My book tour was canceled. I spent a few days being miserable and thinking all my efforts would go to waste. I also spent a lot of time wishing for reality to be different than it was, for the universe to give me a better hand. That's a futile exercise trying to control what can't be controlled.

If you can turn within and ask yourself, 'I cannot change the hand that the universe dealt me, but how can I play the hand I have? What is mine to shape here?'

That's a much more fruitful question to ask. Asking that question led me to come up with creative ways of getting the word out about the book virtually, like doing book launch events with other authors in similar positions, and that changed everything. At that moment, I could just have said, 'My plans have been scuttled. There was nothing I could do,' or there's a much better way of approaching it which I finally did after I crawled out of my canyon of despair which is to ask, 'What can I do with the hand? How can I use my skills and resources in a way that I haven't used them before to solve the problems that need solving right now, as opposed to the problems that I wanted and expected to solve?' That's a much more productive way of looking at the world."

Who knew that launching his book at the height of a pandemic would be perfect timing with a message everyone needed to hear?

Ozan truly believes that *"success won't make you happy. That is a lesson I'm still learning and re-learning because I have been so achievement-oriented my entire life. Initially, it was coming to the US, working on the Mars Rovers Project, and then getting into a great law school and federal clerkship. It was like one mountain after the next. I always thought that happiness was on the other side. Happiness will come once I reach the top of that mountain. But, of course, it doesn't. Once you reach the top of one mountain, you look for others to conquer, and you keep telling yourself, 'I'm going to postpone happiness and the life that I want to create for myself until after this momentous occasion.' That is untrue. Happiness for me lies in those small moments. If you're unhappy before success comes, you won't necessarily be happy after it either."*

Ozan Varol's journey from a small apartment in Istanbul to becoming a rocket scientist, award-winning professor, and best-selling author is remarkable. His belief that obstacles are just stories we tell ourselves made him see beyond perceived limitations. Ozan's experience during the pandemic has also taught him the value of adapting to change and finding creative solutions. On the days you feel challenged by which choice to make, I hope you reflect on Ozan's story and the message that happiness lies in the small moments and the safest path isn't always the best.

Eric Weiner: In Search of Not Knowing

Traveling can be scary. You could get lost with no sense of direction of where you are and no one to talk to. But some people simply enjoy the wanderlust of being in the unknown. They are overly curious people that just want to know more about the world around them.

Eric Weiner is a world traveler and author of the New York Times bestseller *The Geography of Genius*, the critically acclaimed *Man Seeks God, The Geography of Bliss,* and *The Socrates Express: In Search of Life Lessons from Dead Philosophers*, all brilliant books. He is a former foreign correspondent for NPR, and he has reported from more than three dozen countries. His work has appeared in The New Republic, The Atlantic, National Geographic, The Wall Street Journal, The Anthology, and Best American Travel Writing.

When I sat down with Eric, it felt like I was strapping in for a global adventure. Having read his books, I knew he would take me to places I only knew from stories, but I trusted that he was the right person to guide me there.

As a five-year-old boy, he lived with his parents in Towson, Maryland, in what he would call a very unhappy home. He recalls feeling like something was off, which fueled his interest in exploring.

"I suspect something was happening in my five-year-old mind, but at that time, I only knew I wanted to explore. So I set off on a walk and ended up running away from home to explore like Marco Polo. I got far for a five-year-old. I got about two miles from our house. I would have made it to wherever I was trying to go if the Baltimore County Police had not abruptly stopped my expedition. I thought, 'Marco Polo did not have to put up with this crap.' The cops brought me back.

I was curious about what was around the next corner. You can be both running from something and running to something. That's what I was doing. Ever since that moment, if not before, I have had this deep and persistent wondrous wanting to know what's around the next corner. I wanted to see the world."

Eric graduated with a degree in English literature, leading him to a journalism career. He was a foreign correspondent for over a decade and transitioned from being a tourist experiencing the world to reporting on it. Eric had the fantastic opportunity to live in New Delhi, Tokyo, and Jerusalem and traveled to many other countries during his career.

"There are lines about letting go of things not meant for you. The hardest thing is to let go of something good that is almost the right thing for you, but

not quite the right thing. Letting go of that flaming hot torch that's burning in your hand, that's easy to let go of. Letting go of the baseball bat with razor blades is easy. But when you are letting go of a bouquet, but it's not quite the right flowers, it's hard.

This job was close to being what was right for me in terms of creative expression and everything else, but it wasn't quite right because of the negativity bias in journalism, which is baked in. Journalists use a cynical expression: 'If it bleeds, it leads.' The idea is that good news is not news, generally. So I always had a background home of melancholia, low-grade depression, whatever you want to call it. I think being a foreign correspondent, once the initial thrill wore off, this depression was getting worse because I was immersing myself in wars in places like Afghanistan, Iraq, and other places and seeing humanity at its worst – humans doing their worst to other humans.

One day, I had an epiphany: 'Instead of traveling around the world and finding the most miserable people, what if I spend a year traveling to the happiest places, looking for the happiest people and what lessons they could teach us?'"

After this idea came to him, Eric spoke to the NPR correspondent, who thought the idea was utterly ludicrous. Even with pressure from his higher-ups to stay the course and continue reporting negative news, Eric couldn't get the idea out of his head about shifting the narrative, which led to a proposal for his book, *The Geography of Bliss*.

On Eric's journey to discovering the world from a positive perspective, he has learned, *"Happy people don't spend a lot of time analyzing their happiness. They are too busy being happy. The countries that analyze happiness and dissect it are not necessarily the happiest. In the US, we have a cottage industry of self-help books, books about happiness, and the science of happiness, but we are not in the top ten happiest countries in the world. In other countries like Thailand, the Thai have an expression. 'You think too much.' They believe that excessive thinking is a sign of mental illness.*

I had to go on with a completely open mind. I'm open to the idea that everything I think is provisional. People respond to my openness that I'm not coming there with an agenda or to bad mouth their country or whitewash it. I listen. When I was a journalist, an interview was very transactional. Now I'm talking to people. We are having a conversation. There's a shift in attitude. I develop my skills as a deep listener. It has been said that listening is an act of love. I think there's great truth to that. I learned how to love by listening.

Socrates, who was the original converser, would go around ancient Athens. He was curious to talk about big subjects like what's courage. He would go up to a general and say, 'You are a General. You must know what courage is.'

They would have a conversation, but Socrates would keep pressing him, 'You say this, but what about this?' It soon became clear to Socrates that the general had no idea what courage was, and the poet didn't know what beauty was. Socrates comes to the interesting conclusion that 'At least I know that I don't know.'

That is the beginning of all discovery. It is knowing that you don't know. This kind of ignorance, I'm speaking of, is necessary for any creative endeavor or any discovery because if you think you know it all, that's another way of saying you are shut down to new ideas and new ways of thinking.

The first step is called fully conscious ignorance. You know what you don't know and are receptive to seeing new ways of being. My all-time favorite quote about travel is from the writer Henry Miller. He said, 'One's destination is never a place, but a new way of looking at things.' That is my approach to travel and to life. I'm going to try to know and see more. Knowledge is something you possess. It becomes another possession. Wisdom, which I write about in my book, is something you see and do. It has more to do with vision than the accumulation of facts and information."

When we are open to embracing situations from a beginner's mind without preconceived notions of how they should be, it's enlightening. Being open-minded has gifted Eric the ability to find *"incredible overlaps between ancient Greeks in 300 BC and the Buddhist teachings. The beginner's mind is a Buddhist idea, but Buddhism had already been around for 300 years when Socrates said, 'At least I know that I don't know.' We are taught, especially in this country, to be results-oriented. The beginner's mind is not a results-oriented approach to life. You are not looking for results. One of my favorite little nuggets of wisdom comes from the Bhagavad Gita, a revered Hindu spiritual text. Lord Krishna said to Arjuna essentially, 'I will put 100% effort into whatever you are doing but have 0% invested in the results.' If we invest our energy and talents into something, we almost, but not automatically, want to know the results. We want there to be the result. It doesn't work that way. If 2020 has taught us anything, we have far less control over external events now than we thought."*

When Eric transitioned out of his prestigious job as a journalist, he remembers many people questioning his decision. However, by getting out of the hustle and bustle, he had the opportunity to *"reach, in aggregate terms, fewer people with my books, but I reached them more deeply,"* which truly mattered to him.

"Workaholics are rewarded in our culture. You put in the hours at the office. As a result, you get promoted, you make more money, and people think highly of you, but it can be destructive."

Eric Weiner's life journey has been shaped by his insatiable wanderlust and his endless curiosity about the world. From his childhood days of exploring his neighborhood to his career as a foreign correspondent and author, Eric has traveled the globe, seeking to understand the diverse cultures and perspectives that make up our world. His willingness to let go of what is not meant for him and his commitment to embracing situations from a beginner's mind has gifted him with a deep understanding of the world and an ability to reach people on a profound level. By following his passions and staying open to new experiences, Eric has forged a unique path that has allowed him to find happiness and fulfillment and inspire others to do the same.

The Lessons

These leaders have pushed through challenges, judgment, and more to create the life they have today. Looking inward and seeing that we are more powerful than we know can help us acknowledge that taking detours or choosing a path you never thought possible can be one of the best decisions we will ever make.

Ozan Varol's early experiences fostered his curiosity and determination, which led him to a career in astrophysics and beyond. His experiences during the pandemic highlight the value of adaptability and creative problem-solving in the face of adversity. Ultimately, Ozan continues to identify and leave the safety nets on a constant quest to risk his significance and find happiness in the small moments.

Eric Weiner's insatiable curiosity and adventurous spirit led him to explore the world from a young age, ultimately inspiring him to shift his career focus from reporting on human suffering to uncovering the secrets of happiness. By embracing a beginner's mind, staying open to new experiences, and not putting himself in a box, Eric has gained profound insights into diverse cultures and perspectives. His willingness to let go of what wasn't meant for him and invest fully in his passions has not only deepened his impact on readers but also serves as a valuable lesson for others seeking a fulfilling and authentic life.

Questions

As we wrap up Lesson 6, let's circle back to the three C's of grounded leadership: curiosity, compassion, and connection, with some questions for you to ponder and journal.

- What boxes are you currently putting yourself in, and how can you break free from self-imposed limitations?
- Can you identify any unconventional opportunities or experiences in your past that have contributed to your personal or professional growth? How have these experiences shaped who you are today?

- Are there any passions, interests, or skills you have dismissed or neglected because they don't fit your current career path? How can you incorporate these aspects of yourself into your life and work?
- How can you start challenging yourself to think outside the box and be more open to unexpected opportunities? How can you cultivate a mindset of adaptability and growth?

End Notes

I Will Not Die an Unlived Life: Reclaiming Purpose and Passion. Markova, Dawna. Mango Media, 2021

The Bhagavad Gita. Translated by Eliot Deutsch, Holt, Rinehart, and Winston, 1968

Think Like a Rocket Scientist – Ozan Varol

Awaken Your Genius – Ozan Varol

Geography of Genius – Eric Weiner

Geography of Bliss – Eric Weiner

Man Seeks God – Eric Weiner

The Socrates Express – Eric Weiner

Fight For What You Believe In

Success isn't always a linear path. It's easy to get discouraged when things don't go as planned, but the true test of our determination and commitment is whether or not we keep pushing forward despite setbacks. The key to success is to fight for what we believe in, even when the odds are against us. This means putting in the work, staying focused on our goals, and persevering through challenges and obstacles.

Take the example of planting vegetables in a garden. To see the fruits of our labor, we must consistently care for our plants by providing them with the necessary water, light, and nutrients. Of course, we can throw seeds on the ground and hope for the best, but if we are willing to put in the time and effort required to cultivate it, we can expect a more bountiful harvest. Also, we need to be prepared to fight off the weeds that creep in to extract nutrients from our crops.

Similarly, when working toward a personal or professional goal, we must be willing to put in the work and stay committed, even when the going gets tough. We may face setbacks, obstacles, and even failures. It's easy to give up when things don't go as planned, but true champions understand that success requires perseverance and a willingness to fight for what we believe in. If we stay focused on our goals and remain committed to our dreams, we can accomplish great things, even in the face of adversity.

So, don't give up on something that truly matters to you. Instead, embrace the challenges, stay focused on your goals, and keep fighting for what you believe in. Remember, success is not about being perfect; it's about showing up every day, even when it's hard, and staying committed to your dreams.

As we journey through life, we often find ourselves in leadership positions as business owners, managers, or even just as role models for our friends and family. In these positions, we must remember that we are our own harshest critics. We hold ourselves to high standards, and while that can be a good thing, it can also be a double-edged sword.

DOI: 10.4324/9781003364818-8

To become excellent leaders who reach our goals and create incredible lives and businesses for ourselves and those around us, we must cultivate compassion for ourselves and others. We must forgive our missteps and pick ourselves up when we fall. This is not always an easy task, but it is necessary to achieve greatness.

Sometimes, we may find ourselves in situations where we have missed a deadline or failed to meet a goal. It can be tempting to throw in the towel and give up entirely. However, it is crucial to remember that a bad day or week does not have to equal a complete failure. Instead of dwelling on our missteps, we can pick right back up and continue our routine.

You may be frustrated if you miss a day of tending your garden, but it is not catastrophic. And this is an excellent metaphor for how we can approach life's setbacks. Instead of giving up entirely, we get back to our routine. This small act of self-compassion can make all the difference in our overall success.

It is also important to remember that some of the most successful people in the world have launched complete flops or have yet to reach their goals. However, instead of throwing in the towel completely, they saw it through and kept going. This is what defines success – seeing it through no matter what.

By becoming grounded leaders who inspire and motivate others to achieve greatness in their own lives, we learn to cultivate self-compassion and extend compassion to others. We forgive ourselves and others for mistakes and continue to strive for our goals, no matter how difficult the journey may be. Finally, we believe in and champion others while working toward our goals.

The moments when others believed in us stand out in our memories because they fulfill our need for connection and validation. Humans have an inherent desire to feel seen, heard, and understood by others. When someone believes in us, it confirms that we are not alone and that our efforts are not in vain. Moreover, when someone who we look up to or respect believes in us, it can be a powerful motivator. It can give us the courage and confidence to push through challenging times and pursue our goals with renewed vigor.

We must surround ourselves with people who believe in us personally and professionally. We need communities that provide us with constructive feedback, honest reflections, and unwavering support. When we have these types of people in our lives, we can weather the storms of our career paths and come out stronger on the other side.

However, it is also important to be open to positive reinforcement and acknowledge the moments when others believe in us. Sometimes, we can be our own worst critics, and we discount the positive feedback we receive. Instead, we must welcome it and let it nourish us on our journey.

This lesson includes stories of people whose belief in a cause was the driving force that led them to make a significant impact, even in the face of challenging odds. In addition, we will look at the inspiring stories of people who knew what they wanted, consistently worked every day to reach their goals, and learned to pivot instead of stop along the way.

Dolores Hirschmann: Overcoming Self-Doubt and Finding Clarity

Dolores Hirschmann believes ideas can positively impact the world and is passionate about helping entrepreneurs increase their visibility. She is the founder of Masters In Clarity and an internationally recognized strategist, coach, TEDx organizer, and speaker. She is also the author of *Stand Out the TED Way: Be Seen & Grow Your Business.*

I have known Dolores for a while, and I have been blown away by her ability to understand the essence of people's work and their messages. She is a compassionate believer in people and their causes, and I knew she would be the perfect person to feature in this chapter.

"What do you want?" That one question broke Dolores down to tears. *"I was 38 years old, and I started crying. I came home and told my husband about the meeting, where I was asked this very simple question. He didn't say anything. Instead, he showed me that YouTube clip of the movie, A League of Their Own, where Tom Hanks tells Geena Davis, 'There's no crying in baseball.' For me, it was more like, "There's no crying in business, but I definitely cried."*

Every act of rebellion starts with one thought inside a person's head. However, not every fight is about fighting something "out there" in the world. Often, the biggest battle is the internal battle to become the person you want to be by overcoming the negative self-talk of imposter syndrome.

Dolores learned how to help others fight their own internal battles of self-doubt and judgment to get clarity around exactly what they want.

When Dolores was asked the questions that broke her into tears, she was stuck. At that time, she was a mom of four, originally from Argentina, who had started a new company every five years because she wasn't clear on that one question. She described herself as a serial entrepreneur because she loves the art of building and being a part of a team; however, she kept feeling unhappy and unfulfilled.

"At that time, I allowed myself to stay in a situation that was not con-ducive to me being at my best self or my personal and professional growth. Nevertheless, I got sucked into it. I was a hostage of my own confusion."

Every single action reveals the next action. I was fighting my own internal battles of self-doubt and judgment to get clarity about exactly what I wanted. I got curious about this, and it changed everything.

I stopped blaming how I felt about situations that I thought I couldn't control. Instead, it was like, 'Maybe there is some responsibility of mine in this.'"

The signs showed up from then on for Dolores. She heard someone talking about coaching when coaching as an industry wasn't all that well known. That word "coaching" then showed up again in a conversation with her sister later that week, and she followed the crumbs, got curious about the industry, and called a coach to learn more. By January 2013, Dolores was sitting in a room in Boston at the Hyatt, attending the Coaches Training Institute in their certification program. That was a whole new beginning in her life and career.

"We are happy to drive 60 miles per hour on the highway. All we have is our car headlights to show us the way. In every second of driving, the vision is revealed. Every single action reveals the next action."

I loved that analogy because it's true. Our vision is limited only by what's illuminated directly before us. We can't see too far ahead or behind us, but we keep moving forward into the light. As long as we're moving forward, we get to see what the light illuminates next so we know which turns to take, which way the road curves, and what's around the next bend.

"Clarity alone, what's the use of it? You get clear in your head, but who do you serve if you don't take action? What impact do you have if you never show up? It's that breadcrumb, and I have learned to love the reveal. This means we dare and have the courage to follow every step of the process, trusting that whatever is on the other side will be clear and actionable. Every one of the steps reveals the next step."

To replace fear with curiosity, watch as the steps reveal themselves and then act. Before you know it, you will look back and say, "Here I am. I have made those steps. Look at what I have become." Everything looks like a challenge when you are in the middle of the dance.

On the third weekend of Dolores' coaching training, she was asked another impactful question, "What would be your bold action? What would you do if you could not fail?"

"You have to be willing to experience the full range of emotions when you're a leader or entrepreneur because that is where the gifts are hidden."

This leads us to the next big challenge that Dolores had to overcome. Starting her coaching business presented new challenges she had to prepare herself for.

"One of the most challenging endeavors you can take on is building your business, specifically, a personal brand business where you are the product. Talk about self-doubt, lack of confidence, and working your confidence muscle. Even in a normal, uneventful startup phase of my business, it was such an emotional roller coaster. I had a lot of tears and frustration."

Life itself is a rollercoaster. The startup phase that business founders and leaders go through is not for the faint of heart. So when you sign on to become a leader, it's essential to understand that the more you do it and engage in a full range of emotions, the more you become adept at it.

"It's easy to say now, but if I could look back on my path and change anything, I would change the nagging voice of perfection and judgment." Taking action even when you are in fear is the secret to success. It may not be perfect or pretty, but it will keep you moving forward, and that's the goal, forward momentum, and progress over perfection.

Eventually, once you start realizing that the work that you're doing is more significant than the fear, self-doubt, lack of self-worth, or whatever emotion you're experiencing, it's almost like a responsibility and what you owe to the people around you. It becomes a power unto itself that over-rules your fear. As soon as the work becomes bigger than ourselves, we start becoming unstoppable. When I think about my conversation with Dolores, I think of the quote, "When you have a powerful yes, it can overcome any no."

One of the things we talked about was the importance of taking imperfect action. It can be easy to be paralyzed by fear or stuck in a cycle of waiting for perfection, and as a result, you don't move forward. We often have to battle that nagging fear that putting out less than perfection will lead us directly to failure. However, not stepping out into the light won't get us any further.

"I'm going to give you a specific example. When I started, someone said, 'If you're going to build a business, you need to talk to your market and nurture your leads.' So I thought, 'Okay, I need to create a way to com-municate with my mailing list consistently. I will write out a newsletter every week.' It's simple, and so I did for a few months.

I have a dear wonderful neighbor. She is 20 years older than she is the sweetest lady. She emailed me one day, 'Dolores, I admire your work. I love the courage that you have and how you're putting yourself out there. I love you. Please let me edit your newsletters because you have typos and grammatical errors?'

I said yes and was grateful. She was kind about it. The truth is that if I had not done those newsletters with my typos and I had waited to have the money to pay for an editor or learn better English, I don't know what I would have done. Those emails would never have gone out, and the action would never have been taken to grow the business. That's a simple example of progress over perfection."

Dolores shared how she continues to fight the voice of self-doubt as her career has grown and how her perspective has shifted.

"It started to go away when I started building my team. I am leading between nine and ten people now. So it's like a flip in the brain where you start looking at this more objectively and understand that, 'I'm no longer growing a company named Dolores Hirschmann. I am growing a company

named Masters in Clarity. I was in a meeting with them because we're in the middle of changing our brand. So I told my team, I want to hear what you like and don't like because the Masters in Clarity brand is us. It's not me.'

When you start to doubt yourself, your team reminds you what you're doing right. You have clients who believe in you and remind you how you impact them. Self-doubt is a growing pain, but what happens is you start realizing that the work you are doing is bigger than the fear, self-doubt, or lack of self-worth, it still might be there, but it no longer has the power to stop you as it used to."

I asked Dolores if she had any advice for budding entrepreneurs who might feel stuck or confused, and I loved what she shared. *"Don't take action too quickly. Keep on walking until the blisters in your shoes start bleeding. There is a sweet moment when your situation is no longer sustainable. You are feeling a range of emotions. You've got to be uncomfortable to have the courage to shift.*

My best friend growing up was struggling in her career. We would talk weekly about how she hated her job for over a year. I told her, 'I need to ask you a favor.' She said 'Sure.' She would do anything for me. I told her, 'Go outside, open your car door, put your hand between the door and the car, and close the door.' She looked at me like I was crazy. I said, 'Do that because you haven't yet reached the depth of your pain.'

At that moment, I was speaking to her fear of a shift. The blister wasn't just bleeding. It was deforming her foot, and she was still staying stuck there. This masochist invitation got her to shift her perspective. Within months, she quit her job and started to thrive. So basically, my message was, 'Stay super uncomfortable and then change.' If you recognize yourself in that space, this may give you the shift you need."

Dolores Hirschmann is a compassionate and visionary entrepreneur who has battled self-doubt and confusion throughout her journey. Through her experiences, she learned the power of taking imperfect action, embracing change, and trusting the process. Let us remember that our greatest battles often lie within ourselves. Yet, we can grow and find clarity by overcoming our fears, self-doubt, and judgment. You are not alone on this path; with each step, you will gain the strength and wisdom needed to create a meaningful impact in the world.

Bob Coughlin: Riding the Waves on a Journey to Impact

Some of us have a clear plan for our life's path, navigating through education and career goals, but sometimes, life happens, and our plans fall through. That is why Bob Coughlin is a great believer in not overthinking, which led him to become far beyond the person he had planned to become and is now impacting so many lives.

From a politician to the president and CEO of MassBio to managing director of Life Sciences at JLL, where he is a valued partner to life science companies, Bob has worked diligently to make Massachusetts better by getting the life sciences ecosystem and government to work together. Bob has profoundly impacted the industry, but his true impact is felt far beyond Massachusetts.

Anyone who has worked in the life sciences industry knows Bob, and he is so well known that you don't even have to say his last name, and people know who you are talking about. Anytime I heard him speak at an event, I left feeling energized and inspired because I knew he cared deeply and spoke with passion and perseverance. He is a true believer.

And through it all, Bob's journey is about riding the waves and finding the compass to his life's work. Bob grew up the youngest of six boys. He went to the Massachusetts Maritime Academy, where he fell in love with student government. He got elected to be a student member of the board of trustees. As a result, Bob became a student member of the board of regents representing all 29 colleges and universities in Massachusetts.

While at Mass Maritime, he couldn't go on the semester at sea because he participated in student government during his senior year. So while he was home, his dad said, "You're a good kid, but you're not going to live in my house for two months without having a job or doing something productive. So what are you going to do?"

Bob had looked for a job but couldn't find anything, but his dad mentioned that he could run for the school committee in the town of Dedham, Massachusetts. His dad was a selectman for a long time in the town, so people knew him. So at age 19, he decided to run for the school committee and won. He jokingly said, *"Everyone thought they were voting for my dad. So that's how I got into politics."*

Bob went back to college to finish and graduate but then couldn't ship out in the Merchant Marines because he had two years left in his term as a member of the school committee in Dedham. So instead, he got an entry-level job at a startup at the time called Clean Harbors Environmental Services.

Bob felt that democracy wasn't being served in his district by the existing state representative, so he decided to challenge the seated state representative, the assistant majority leader in the House of Representatives. Unfortunately, there was less than a 1% chance of knocking out an incumbent at the time in the Commonwealth, but Bob decided to become a full-time politician.

While that was happening, life took an unexpected turn. Bob's wife was pregnant with their third child while he was running for the House. During a standard pregnancy screening, they discovered that the unborn baby would have cystic fibrosis. Bob was 30 years old at the time with two kids, a beautiful wife, and running for the legislature. Their whole world was changed forever in that moment.

"They told us that we had an unborn baby that would be born with an expiration date. You can only imagine what that does to you emotionally and psychologically. It's tragic."

After extensive research, they met with genetic counselors, Boston Children's Hospital, and the Cystic Fibrosis (CF) Foundation. He immediately decided to leave the race, return to work, and care for his family. However, while going through that process, he met some fantastic social workers and counselors at Boston Children's Hospital. One of the counselors got him thinking about how much good he could do for sick people if he were a lawmaker that cared about drug discovery and patient care. That was a real eye-opener for him.

Bob stayed the course, remained in the race, got elected, and started spending a significant amount of time working with leaders of the life science industry, talking about the intersection of policy and innovation. Bob became the go-to person in the House for the biotech industry early in this stage of the game. He led the debate on somatic cell nuclear transfer, which is embryonic stem cell research. He also championed a ten-year billion-dollar life science initiative that put this industry on the map.

Bob was trying to change laws to make Massachusetts better for the life sciences while working with the Cystic Fibrosis Foundation and The Joey Fund to focus on developing a cure for his son. *"Joe* (founder of the Joey Fund, which supports patient care and research*) came to me in the hospital the day my son was born and said, 'Why don't we raise $100 million and invest it in our own company, so your kid doesn't die as my Joey did. We're going to buy a cure for your kid.'"*

Bob learned everything about the industry from a policy and capital formation standpoint. As a result, Little Bobby was in six clinical trials before he was even six years old. He learned how the system was broken, leading him to leave the legislature to join the Deval Patrick administration, where they passed the life science initiative that boosted the industry and catalyzed the work of many promising therapies.

There were a lot of ups and downs along the way, but Bob felt like he never really chose his career; it chose him. During his career at MassBio, after 18 years and $13 billion invested, Vertex Pharmaceuticals developed and launched a drug called Trikafta that keeps his son alive today. Since he has been on that medication, he has grown 8 inches, gained 50 pounds, and his lung function is back to what it was when he was five years old. Just three decades ago, the average person with cystic fibrosis would live only to the age of 30, but now 50 years is typical.

"Sometimes our careers and lives are like the ocean, and our path has been nothing but riding on waves. Then, suddenly, you find the compass setting, and you move at a rapid speed. You see the wind, and you go at it. There are rough waters, but you go forth purposefully and steer toward your

destination. It will serve you well. After all, smooth seas never made a skilled sailor. You wouldn't enjoy the smooth seas if you didn't have rocky seas. You wouldn't know they were good. We wouldn't know the sunny days if we didn't have rainy days. So take it in, feel it, deal with it, and work through it."

You will never hit the snooze button again if you feel driven by a meaningful purpose. You want to get up every day and attack it. Something terrible happened to Bob's family, but it can change your view entirely if you look at all the good it did. Anyone who's going through adversity, remember, "It can't rain forever."

On November 9, 2019, Bobby got his first dose of Trikafta. While Bob had a few years left in his final contract at MassBio, he ultimately decided that life is short, fragile, and precious, and while he loved the job, he was ready for his next journey with less stress and more enjoyment.

"Being put in a situation you do not have much control over can be humbling. Anything is possible. Nothing is impossible. You can get the right people pulled together if there are complicated problems. That's where diversity comes in. The more diverse any group, the better the scientific outcome is. Never give up. We need some key elements to make things possible: purpose, passion, resilience, and persistence. You don't give up when your kid's life is at stake. I have learned that anything is possible. That's a lesson that I share with everybody.

In hindsight, the advice that I would give to other people is that your work is something that you do during the day. It's important. It helps you pay the bills. If you're passionate about it, even better, but don't ever sacrifice those beautiful moments that don't happen for long periods of time. You must have that balance and moderation."

Bob Coughlin's journey demonstrates the power of embracing the unexpected and adjusting to the rough waters of life. Through hardship and perseverance, Bob found a deep sense of purpose in his work and life, ultimately making a meaningful impact on the lives of countless people. His story is a testament to the importance of staying resilient and using life's challenges as opportunities for growth and positive change. By finding the compass setting amid life's storms, we can navigate through rough waters and emerge as skilled sailors, ready to tackle our next adventure with purpose, passion, and determination. As Bob so eloquently said, "It can't rain forever." So embrace the unexpected and let it guide you to a life of fulfillment and purpose.

Franziska Iseli: Embrace Your Inner Rebel on the Path to Entrepreneurial Success

Embrace your inner rebel and learn how to carve your own path to success. Franziska Iseli did just that. Like a rebel, she has started numerous companies, championed many environmental causes, and even rode a motorbike from Switzerland to Kazakhstan. Franziska is the best-selling author of the incredible book *The Courage Map: 13 Principles for Living Boldly.* As an entrepreneur, marketing strategist, and winner of the 2013 Young Entrepreneur of the Year award, she has co-founded several companies, including Basic Bananas, Moments of Humanity, The Business Hood, and Oceanlovers.

Even though Franziska lives and works in Australia, a 15-hour time difference from where I live, we had the absolute pleasure of working together on many exciting projects. She believes anything is possible if you have the courage to get uncomfortable. Her sense of adventure and willingness to explore new things is a catalyst for taking bold action.

In anyone's life, there are pivot points that change everything. With most journeys, there are always a few crossroads where you can either go left or right. Sometimes you're led to a fascinating place or interesting people, or sometimes you wish you had taken the other turn!

The most significant pivot point in Franziska's life was many years ago when her father died unexpectedly of a heart attack at 58. At the time, she was working at an advertising agency doing strategy for big clients. Upon her father's death, she looked at her life and suddenly realized she was mortal. *"I asked myself, what if I died right now? Would I be happy with what I'm doing and with what I'm achieving for people?"*

Franziska realized she could do more and have a more significant impact if she went out on her own, so she left her career and started her first business, Basic Bananas. Basic Bananas is a marketing education company that provides small business owners, entrepreneurs, and marketing professionals with the knowledge, tools, and strategies to effectively market their products or services. The company aims to empower businesses to create powerful marketing strategies by simplifying complex concepts and making them easy to understand and implement. Check them out to hear the story behind their quirky name.

When she started the business in 2009, Franziska had a business mentor because she knew marketing, advertising, and branding but needed to learn how to run an actual business. The mentor advised against calling the business Basic Bananas.

"Sharon, I will take a lot of your advice," Franziska said, *"but not this one because I know branding; this is my strength. I know I can make this work with the name Basic Bananas."*

As she got going, she realized she could profoundly impact the world through entrepreneurship. There's an element of being a rebel that runs through all of the decisions she has made. When Franziska feels something in her gut, she makes the decision, and only later will people usually see that she was right. Being a rebel and carving out her own path has served her and her businesses well.

The first eight months in business were quite challenging. She had to learn bookkeeping, paying taxes, invoicing, managing clients, implementing systems, and creating websites. But, always one to play by her strengths and outsource her weaknesses, she knew she'd be able to grow this business a lot quicker if she focused on what she was good at.

Franziska now has a team of more than 30 people in different countries and operations on different continents, and the same initial principles still apply. That is, *"Always lead with value. How can we add value? How can we provide something epic for people?"* That was her sole focus in the formative months of her business, staying focused on helping people. In the beginning, she was doing a lot of pro-bono work to get case studies and show people the results. Then, it started to snowball and gain momentum.

Once you start, you have to be consistent. Franziska's first mentoring program had three people sitting in the workshop. One was her mother-in-law, and one was her friend. *"Only one person could have been a potential customer, and of course, they didn't become a customer. Seven people showed up in the next session; the next one, we had ten. Eventually, we had hundreds of people. It's just consistency and always leading with value. It's about showing up for yourself, your teams, and your customers.*

One of our key principles, which I've embraced from the beginning, is embracing failures. If we never fail, it means we're not trying hard enough. So be okay with failures and don't beat yourself up. I never beat myself up about failures and I fail a lot. I don't even have examples because I don't see it as a failure. I have tried, and this didn't work, but I have learned something. I want my team to do the same."

Franziska believes it all comes back to mindset and has always been fascinated by human psychology, so she did some social experiments of her own. For example, she ran the New York City marathon without training to see if her mindset would be enough to finish (she finished in four hours!).

There was also the time when Franziska had the crazy idea to travel by motorcycle around the Middle East. She calls it her *"best, worst idea, and I have many of them."* But she said, *"How can I push myself harder? How can I push myself mentally, physically, and emotionally harder?"*

Franziska wanted to grow more. She knew she could push herself a little more and wanted to do something big, scary, and a little crazy. She considered climbing Mount Kilimanjaro or Mount Everest, but the cold was too much of a barrier. Then she recalled something she had read about Marco Polo, the Italian merchant in ancient Italy who traveled along the Silk Road from Italy to the Middle East and into Asia.

She thought, *"What if I ride a motorbike from Switzerland, my home country, into Kazakhstan and through Iran? This would be an interesting experiment because it will be challenging on many levels, especially physically."*

The journey led to her book, *The Courage Map*. Two things came out of her trip; the first one was the principles of courage and how to apply them. The second one was the moments of pure humanity that led her to a movement to connect strangers through kindness. Franziska found infinite moments on this journey where total strangers were kind, helping her, taking her in and offering a bed in their house, giving her tea, helping with food, or anything that she needed help with. People were kind.

We're all human and can accept each other exactly how we are, regardless of religion, and that is a lesson Franziska learned on her journey. She traveled to many predominantly Muslim countries like Turkey, Tajikistan, and Uzbekistan. Although Franziska isn't particularly religious and wasn't wearing a scarf, she was riding a motorbike, which women in some countries don't do, and people welcomed her with open arms. She never had anyone that wasn't nice because of her different cultural or religious background.

"One kid told me a little bit about his religion and Allah. And then he asked me about my religion, and I said, I believe in stars, bees, sunshine, the universe, and the ocean.' He completely accepted it, which was amazing to witness."

I asked her what advice she had to share with others on their life journey. Her reply was beautiful: *"We need to take the shots. There's a quote that I'm paraphrasing by Michael Jordan along the lines of, 'I will only ever fail the shots I didn't take.' It's the same with life. I felt the same about my journey. It's about taking chances, just trying and going for it. As I mentioned earlier, it's okay if it doesn't work. Failure is okay. We should be able to make mistakes and forgive ourselves.*

The second thing is that it is okay to be imperfect. Perfection isn't an excuse not to take action. Sometimes we wait for perfection; we strive for perfection, and it stops us from starting something.

The third thing is one of the most challenging for me: the principle of non-attachment. We need to be unattached to the outcome. Why? Because we don't know what's coming for us.

2020 was unpredictable. If we were attached to certain outcomes, goals, and things we wanted to achieve, we would have been let down. Rather than getting attached to these outcomes, I recommend only focusing on what you can change and what you are in control of, which is how you respond, act, and behave. You can't control if there's another pandemic, the market changes, or what the weather will be. I cannot waste my energy on stuff I have zero control over."

Franziska Iseli's journey demonstrates the power of embracing your inner rebel and daring to carve a unique path to success. Franziska has built a thriving career and a remarkable life by consistently pushing her limits, taking bold action, and remaining open to new experiences. Her fearless approach to entrepreneurship and life challenges us to confront our fears, embrace our failures, and take imperfect action toward our goals. So, as you forge your own path, remember to embrace your inner rebel and have the courage to make your own decisions.

The Lessons

Being open to change can help us understand that taking detours or choosing a path we never thought possible can be one of the best decisions we will ever make.

Dolores Hirschmann faced and overcame self-doubt and confusion throughout her career. She teaches the importance of taking imperfect action, embracing change, and trusting the process to find clarity and success. As we fight our limiting beliefs, we must remember that our most significant battles often lie within ourselves. Her analogy of car headlights while driving at night and how we can be moving really fast but only see so far into the future or behind us is a great way to think about how we navigate life. We make decisions based on what we see around us and adjust accordingly, and most importantly, we keep moving forward.

Bob Coughlin's journey from politician to CEO of MassBio to managing director of Life Sciences at JLL highlights the importance of embracing life's unexpected turns and the power of fighting for what you believe in. We don't always know what life will throw at us, and life threw a curveball at Bob. Some people would shut down at that point and become resigned to their fate. Instead, Bob decided he could make a meaningful change through his skills and connections and by joining forces with others in the same boat. There's a huge ripple effect that came from Bob using his talents to help his own son and, in doing so, helped improve the quality of life for many others.

Franziska Iseli's story is all about embracing your inner rebel and daring to forge a unique path to success. Her fight was not only against the status quo but also to pursue her wild dreams, no matter how unconventional they may have seemed to others. Anything is possible when we step out of our comfort zones and persistently chase our aspirations.

Questions

As we wrap up Lesson 7, let's circle back to the three C's of grounded leadership: curiosity, compassion, and connection, with some questions for you to ponder and journal.

- Can you think of a time when someone believed in you, and it significantly impacted your life?

- What is a cause or belief that you are truly passionate about? How can you start taking steps to fight for it?
- Can you recall a time when you fought for something you believed in? What did you learn from that experience, and how can you apply that knowledge moving forward?
- How can you create a support network of like-minded individuals who share your passion for fighting for what you believe in?

End Notes

A League of Their Own. Directed by Penny Marshall, TM & © Sony 1992
  I've missed more than 9000 shots in my career... ... " (Michael Jordan)
  Stand out the TED Way – Dolores Hirschmann
  The Courage Map – Franziska Iseli

Take the Courageous Leap

You have heard the saying that life begins outside your comfort zone. This statement is true and powerful. However, it's not enough to just acknowledge it; action is required. Taking the courageous leap requires you to step out of your comfort zone and into the unknown. It can be a daunting prospect, but it is necessary to achieve your full potential. This chapter will explore the importance of taking measured risks, playing a bigger game, and making a bigger impact.

Taking a risk does not mean a blind leap of faith. Taking measured risks is essential, which includes assessing the potential consequences and making informed decisions. Calculated risks can lead to growth, both personally and professionally. They can help you build your confidence and resilience and expand your skills and knowledge. On the other hand, if you always play it safe, you may miss out on opportunities that could lead to greater success and fulfillment.

In his book, *Thinking, Fast, and Slow*, Nobel Prize-winning psychologist Daniel Kahneman explains that we are often biased toward avoiding loss over seeking gain. This means we may be more likely to stay in our comfort zone, even if it means missing out on potential opportunities. However, we can overcome this bias by taking measured risks and opening ourselves up to new possibilities, for example, starting a new business, applying for a job outside our field, or taking on a leadership role in a new organization.

When you take the courageous leap, you are playing a bigger game. You are stepping out of your comfort zone and into a realm of possibilities. It can be scary to step out of your comfort zone, but it's necessary to achieving extraordinary results. Setting big goals is essential for success. Most people aim too low and consequently achieve mediocre results. By setting bigger goals, you get to push yourself to think outside the box and come up with creative solutions to achieve them.

Taking the courageous leap means expanding your horizons and making a bigger impact on the world. You are contributing your unique talents and gifts, which can have a positive ripple effect on those around you. When you

DOI: 10.4324/9781003364818-9

play it safe, you are not fully utilizing your potential. Taking the courageous leap allows you to make a bigger impact and leave a lasting legacy.

Vulnerability is also essential for making a meaningful impact. When we allow ourselves to be vulnerable and share our true selves, we can connect with others on a deeper level and make a positive impact by volunteering for a charity, starting a non-profit organization, or mentoring others. We can show others the leaps we took and encourage them to take their own.

How does taking the courageous leap connect with the three C's of grounded leadership? Taking the leap involves letting go of the safety and security of what is familiar and embracing the uncertainty of what lies ahead. While this can be scary, it is often necessary for personal growth and transformation.

Curiosity is a critical ingredient in taking the courageous leap. When we approach new experiences with an open and curious mindset, we can be receptive to new ideas, perspectives, and possibilities. We can feel more confident and empowered as we navigate the unknown. Consider this the exploration phase of your leap – where might you land? How long will it take you to get there? What are the possible outcomes? Are there more leaps to come after? What could go wrong? What could go right? Curiosity is a great antidote to fear; it helps us remove our judgments or assumptions and lean into possibility.

When we are compassionate with ourselves, we are more likely to give ourselves permission to take risks and make mistakes. We recognize that failure does not reflect our worth as human beings but rather is an opportunity for growth and learning. When we are compassionate with others, we build connections that can provide support and encouragement as we take the courageous leap.

We need to feel connected to something greater than ourselves in order to find meaning and purpose in our lives. This can take many forms – from connecting with our values and sense of purpose to connecting with a community of like-minded individuals who share our goals and aspirations. Connect with what you really want, who you really want to be, and the life you want to live to help you navigate your leap!

Combining curiosity, compassion, and connection creates a powerful foundation for the courageous leap. We can become more resilient and adaptable if we are willing to take risks to pursue our dreams. And while there are no guarantees in life, we can trust that we have the strength and resources to navigate whatever challenges may come our way.

This lesson includes stories of people who took a courageous leap to step outside their comfort zone and take on new challenges. By taking measured risks, playing a bigger game, and making a bigger impact, they unlocked their potential and created a fulfilling life that has impacted not only themselves but many others.

Bill Harris: Architecting a Path to Embrace Change and Inspiration

Letting go of everything to start a business can be a scary leap most people would not take. But letting go of a company you created can be twice as scary. These are two of the most significant decisions Bill Harris has had to make in his journey.

Bill is a managing director in the New York office of Perkins+Will, an international architecture and design firm. He is a nationally recognized design leader in the life sciences industry and is at the forefront of a trend known as "convergence." That's when traditionally distinct design themes overlap, blend, and blur. Unsurprisingly, he's just as comfortable leading the design of a science laboratory as he is in a workplace, a healthcare environment, or a place for higher learning. Bill loves to surround himself with adventurous thinkers. As a managing director and a design practitioner, he constantly seeks out ways to bring people from different disciplines together. His motto? "Make it work, and make it inspire."

I have had the pleasure of working with Bill on several projects during my time in industry, and working with him was always inspiring. He is a great collaborator who knows when to step back and when to lean in to ensure the project and the people working on it get what they need to be successful.

During our conversation, he walked me through several flashpoints in his career: from discovering his love for architecture to starting his own architectural firm, to being introduced to the power of biotechnology, and being recruited into one of the world's leading architectural design firms, Perkins+Will. Each shift in Bill's journey allowed him to unlock more innovation and possibilities. As he explains, learning how to find his niche was something he would gladly give everything up to pursue.

Bill started his own architectural firm in 1989, the same year he and his wife bought a home and had their first child. Bill grew his business out of his attic; he went from two incomes and apartment living to a mortgage and no fixed income. His journey combined the desire to surround himself with bright and adventurous thinkers, focusing on blending and blurring different disciplines and a battle to avoid micromanagement.

When we talk about making a courageous leap, many people balk because they wonder if they have what it takes. The biggest takeaway from my conversation with Bill is that he actually has a formula, even though he didn't call it that. It came up when I asked him for his book recommendations, one of my favorite questions to ask my guests. One of his recommendations is a book by Bryan Stevenson called *Just Mercy: A Story of Justice & Redemption,* about the case of Walter McMillian, who was convicted and sentenced to death for a crime he did not commit. He talked about inviting the author to speak at his synagogue and how impactful and spellbinding his lecture was. He shared his awe and admiration for his life journey: *"A vision and desire to see that things can be different, a belief that he can make change happen, and then the action to follow up on it."*

As soon as he said it, my brain made it into a math formula: Motivation = a vision and desire to see that things can be different + a belief in the ability to make change happen + the action to follow up on it. You can't work in biotech for as long as I did and not love formulas. It's kind of a job requirement, or so I am told.

Bill started our conversation by talking about growing up in a small town in Vermont and traveling to Montreal to visit his mom's side of the family. He talked about how he watched out the window on these trips as the landscape went from green mountains to flat land to finally, a glittery city slowly coming into view. This was where his love of architecture was born and created excitement about the idea that something out there was waiting to be discovered and experienced. His city-born mother was an artist, and his father was a country-born businessman. This instilled in him a duality by combining a business sense and the ability to be an artistic visionary.

"My superpower is combining business and art and seeing everything almost simultaneously from the artistic, visionary, aesthetic, and business sides. It is not exclusive to me, but it is one of the things that has helped me in my career. I see things from all sides. At the same time, I was doing that in a way that connected different things. – people, businesses, opportunities, industries, places, and food combinations. I love to cook. It infuses an entire perspective on the world. It's the thing that excites me most about what I do. It is making those connections.

In a way, innovation is seeing connections and opportunities that other people don't see. This thinking framed my journey and was a consistent theme in my career. For example, in your introduction, you described where I am now and that I had started my own business. I did that because I had a vision of something I wanted to accomplish that I couldn't quite do where I was. It wasn't that it was bad where I was, but it was just not aligned with me.

People didn't share my enthusiasm and excitement for opportunity and innovation. One of the things that's a real challenge in architecture is being able to respond to two masters. There's the design muse, and then there's the financial driver. We have many architects out there who are 'starchitects.' They create beautiful work, but could care less for the client and the oper-ation. And then there are architects out there who can deliver super eco-nomically, but they have no vision.

You can and should have both. You should be able to do both. I left my employer in 1989 because I wanted to accomplish that mission and move it forward. I didn't see a path there, so I made a move. I didn't intend to start a business, but it became the best option. I was in a holding pattern for a while between jobs because I wasn't sure I wanted the responsibility of running my own business."

Bill took the courageous leap to start his business and learned some important lessons early in his journey. First, he realized that he enjoyed working for himself. So many people fear stepping out of their comfort zones because they fear the unknown and the pressure of running a business. The second thing he realized was that he didn't have to know it all to make it work. He could rely on consultants and peers to fill in any knowledge gaps or even outsource pieces if needed.

I am reminded of the story he told about entering Montreal out of darkness and coming into the light, and it is a great way to explain Bill's gifts, getting people to see things through his eyes. It's part of that connection he creates between where people are, whether they're coming from a business or art discipline, and then bringing it to the other side to be that bridge. It makes me think about design in general and how people underestimate how much design impacts their world. He realized early on that his clients valued not only the functionality and technicality of his designs but also the creativity and aesthetics of the environments he creates.

Over the years, Bill watched his fledgling firm grow, with his wife joining him to take on the business side of things. As a result, he employed top architects and built a solid reputation for mixing function and quality design.

Bill soon found himself specializing in science and biotechnology spaces, an up-and-coming and newly thriving industry. Eventually, with a team of outstanding architects, he was outgrowing his office. But, while he was pondering his next steps, an offer came his way, giving him yet another opportunity to take a courageous leap. That's when one of the world's leading architectural design firms, Perkins+Will, came calling. They saw a future in life science and asked Bill and his whole practice to lead the science team.

I see so much courage in each leap. Every move he took required bravery, and every leap unlocked even more innovation and possibilities. When I asked if he had any regrets, his reply came with the wisdom of someone who could see how things worked out perfectly in hindsight.

"If I made missteps, they prepared me for the next corner. There are no regrets. Every promise of opportunity has played itself out."

What I love about Bill's story is that he didn't wake up with an exact plan for his life. Instead, he tapped into that inner sense that it was time to take a move and stayed open to the opportunities coming his way. Returning to the formula he shared, his vision was finding that sweet spot between form and function. As a result, he was able to capitalize on the biotech industry because he focused on learning and delved into understanding what made lab and tech spaces functional. Courageous leaps aren't always planned or easy to navigate. Bill tapped into his intuition to know when and how to jump!

From starting his architectural firm to joining Perkins+Will, Bill Harris' ability to embrace new opportunities has allowed him to flourish personally and professionally. His story highlights the significance of taking courageous leaps and trusting your intuition, even when the path forward may seem uncertain. The lessons we can learn from Bill's experiences demonstrate that taking risks and pushing beyond our comfort zones can lead to immense growth, innovation, and fulfillment. We can unlock new possibilities and achieve success by embracing change and trusting our instincts, and staying aligned with what truly lights us up.

Tatiana Poliakova: Navigating Adversity With Courage and Intuition

Adversity can make or break a person; having high emotional intelligence and intuition often means the difference between success and failure. Tatiana Poliakova grew up behind the Iron Curtain, and this early experience impacted her significantly. As a result, she has had a remarkable journey from humble beginnings to international banking to helping people transform themselves. Before becoming an executive coach, Tatiana spent over 23 years in leadership positions in investment banking and management consulting.

What inspired me to include Tatiana in this lesson about taking courageous leaps was that she talks about inner and outer courage through her different experiences. Through outer courage, she tackles situations by taking action and staying open to opportunities. Inner courage is the ability to get in touch with your feelings, have humility about your shortcomings to be open for improvement, and shift the narratives inside your head in order to shift your perspective.

Our conversation began with Tatiana recounting a painful early childhood experience. Throughout her story, she vacillates from the profound sadness of her childhood and the lighthearted laughter of her adult self, who can recognize the absurdity of the situation and the lesson it taught her.

She recalls seeing her mother walking down the street during winter in Russia, her face streaked with tears. Her mother was crying because a teacher called her to discuss Tatiana's performance in German class. She even asked her mom if she had trauma during her birth because her progress with the German language had been so disappointing.

"It was a painful moment. It was also the moment I realized the impact that particular behaviors could have on how others perceive you. I'm very

blessed that I have a stepfather who was one of the leading rocket scientists in Russia. When my mom came home upset and shared the news, he said, 'Don't worry, she's intelligent and she is going to graduate with honors, you will see.'"

Young Tatiana accepted the challenge head-on. With the support of her family and her own rebellious nature to prove herself, she did graduate with honors. She went on to study International Economic Affairs in Germany, one of the few women able to do so. At that point, the Soviet Union had fallen, and she was an 18-year-old girl who would previously not have been allowed in such a program under Soviet rule. Determined, she sent multiple letters and received many no's, but ultimately landed a scholarship to study in Germany.

Her next flashpoint happened during her time in Germany. This speaks to another aspect of taking a courageous leap: many of us can get so focused on our destination that we miss out on opportunities put on our path to help us.

"I was thrilled to have an opportunity to interview for a management trainee program at Dresdner Bank. Even though I was still studying in the German program, they gave me a chance based on my Russian degree. Many Germans who have PhDs would go through the selection process. They had never had anyone from the former Soviet Union block in that program. I remember I was on a train to Frankfurt to attend the selection testing, surrounded by books.

This nice elderly man sat beside me and said, 'I see you're reading a lot of finance books.' I said, 'Yes, I have this very important interview.' I was getting a bit irritated because he was distracting me. He says, 'Can I give you some advice? There is another cabin, and we can have lunch in a cafe and talk. I will guarantee you that our conversation will be more helpful to you than those books.' I wanted to say no, but luckily at that moment, I listened to this sense of intuition within me. So I went and had lunch with him.

To my surprise, he was the CEO of a Mittelstand German business (Mittelstand is a German term that refers to small and medium-sized enterprises). *He prepared me for the interview. It's almost as if he knew what they would be asking me, how I should respond, how to show up. He coached me on being authentic and courageous. I still remember exiting the train; he wished me goodbye and good luck. I wouldn't have gotten that job without that memorable encounter on the train."*

That story is powerful for so many reasons. First, you must have the courage to open yourself up to something new and realize that one conversation can open up a world of possibilities. She could have said, "No, I don't want to be distracted. I'm doing the work I need to do, so I don't break my concentration." Instead, she noticed her intuition was telling her something else. It opened up a door to something even bigger. So many people go through life and don't look at the clues that intuition leaves; instead, they just keep their heads down and say, "I'm doing this. Don't bother me."

Leaning on and learning to trust your intuition comes through accumulating and reflecting on experiences.

"There are many occasions in my life where I went more into the habitual behavior of just pushing and persevering. At that moment, I was able to connect with my intuition and my ability to connect with intuition, not just those moments which life presents to you. It's noticing the opportunities. It's also a muscle that we can develop. I'm more consciously looking for these situations."

Along her journey, Tatiana moved to the United States and had a 20-year career in investment banking and working on the trading floor. However, she was at a crossroads after so many years in that arena. Throughout her career, people often came to her to discuss their challenges. As she listened to the stories of her co-workers and even managers, she wondered what drives people and creates this outward success while they felt so depleted on the inside. What differentiates success-empty people from successful ones? How do we build a life that gives us fulfillment and the feeling that we are making an impact and helps us grow in our connections?

At this point, she knew she was ready to take yet another courageous leap. On the trading floor, she had a lot of adrenaline in closing deals, but it started to fade away. She could close a $10 million deal and not feel excited anymore.

What excited her was understanding what drives people and how to support them in leading them in life. It was a challenging decision because she had a comfortable position as the managing director on a trading floor then. There were only seven female managing directors among 300 men in the organization, and she was promoted while working only four days a week. It felt like a super cushy job she could do with her eyes closed.

"It was not an easy decision. But finally, I realized I had to choose joy and passion above comfort."

Herein lies the issue that many people face. They get so tied up, handcuffed by the fear of leaving something comfortable and venturing into the great unknown to create something new. However, Tatiana learned a valuable lesson that she applies to all situations in her life today:

"The most important lesson is realizing how we create our world from the inside out. I remember when I was frustrated, I would come home on a difficult day. It's easy to go into the blame mentality – blaming the market, the trader, the client, the aggressive hedge fund guy or girl, or whoever. The realization I got very early on in my journey as a coach was that I could choose the perspective on how I view the world. The world is created through the story I tell myself.

You can use your energy to create something driven by your intention, or you can use it for anger and disappointment. You can spiral up or spiral down; it is your choice."

She talks about how it's easier to see these spirals in others than in yourself, so getting into the practice of noticing what you have going on internally is an important skill to develop. Tatiana believes in living life from the viewpoint of surrendering. Not in the way of giving up, but in the way that things won't always go as planned, and often, when you surrender, you are open to opportunities. She talked about that moment on the train, the one moment she chose to say yes to an opportunity for a conversation with a stranger that led to her landing an important job that set her on her career path.

We don't always know what is waiting for us around the corner or what opportunities we will say yes to that will lead us on a fantastic journey if only we can stay open enough to recognize them.

Tatiana Poliakova's journey from growing up behind the Iron Curtain to reaching the heights of international banking and becoming an executive coach is remarkable. Her story emphasizes the importance of emotional intelligence, intuition, and the courage to take leaps in the face of adversity. By staying open to opportunities and surrendering to the unknown, Tatiana demonstrated the power of inner and outer courage in navigating life's challenges. Our choices and perspectives can dramatically impact our success and fulfillment. Tatiana's story is an inspiring reminder that embracing our intuition, trusting our instincts, and stepping out of our comfort zones can lead to incredible growth and transformation.

The Lessons

Taking the courageous leap looks different for everyone, but by taking measured risks, playing a bigger game, and making a bigger impact, we can unlock our potential and create a fulfilling life that has impacted not only ourselves, but many others.

For Bill Harris, taking a courageous leap has been a recurring theme in his career. From starting his own architectural firm to letting go of it, Bill has continuously taken brave steps that have unlocked innovation and possibilities. One key lesson from Bill's journey is his formula for motivation: a vision and desire to see things differently, a belief in the ability to make change happen, and the action to follow up on it. He also learned that he didn't have to know it all to make his business work. His story shows that taking courageous leaps isn't always planned or easy, but it can lead to new opportunities and growth.

Tatiana Poliakova's inspiring journey from humble beginnings in Soviet Russia to international banking and executive coaching is a testament to the power of inner and outer courage. Through her experiences, she learned that adversity could make or break a person, and having high emotional intelligence and intuition can be the difference between success and failure. Tatiana shares the importance of being open to opportunities, listening to intuition, and surrendering to the unknown. She also emphasizes the significance of creating your world from the inside out, choosing your perspective, and noticing what's going on internally. These stories remind us to take courageous leaps, even when they are uncomfortable, and to trust that the universe will guide you to where you need to be.

Questions

As we wrap up Lesson 8, let's circle back to the three C's of grounded leadership: curiosity, compassion, and connection, with some questions for you to ponder and journal.

• In what ways can taking the courageous leap make a bigger impact on the world? What impact would you like to make in the world?
• Reflect on a moment when you faced a significant challenge or obstacle. How did you respond, and what did you learn from that experience?
• Identify an area where you feel the need to take a courageous leap. What has been holding you back, and what steps can you take to overcome those barriers?
• Envision the person you want to become after taking a courageous leap. What qualities, skills, or experiences will define this new version of yourself?

End Notes

Thinking, Fast, and Slow – Daniel Kahneman
Just Mercy – Bryan Stevenson

Stay Curious and Evolve as You Grow

Life is an ongoing journey that presents opportunities and challenges at every turn. The journey may seem like a straight line for some, while it might be filled with twists and turns for others. But, regardless of your path, one thing is certain – you will continue to grow and evolve as you gain new experiences.

Some people take divergent paths on their journey. For them, breaking the routine is just how they are wired. They constantly seek new experiences, challenge themselves, and push beyond their limits. These people are often referred to as explorers, and they are the ones who make discoveries that shape the world we live in today. These people adopt what I call an explorer's mindset, a mindset that is open to new experiences and challenges, even in the face of fear.

At its core, the explorer's mindset is about curiosity and a willingness to take risks. It involves stepping outside your comfort zone and trying new things, even if you are unsure of the outcome. It is about embracing the unknown and trusting that you have the skills and resources to navigate whatever comes your way.

One such explorer is Sir Richard Branson, the founder of Virgin Group. Branson has been an advocate of staying curious and evolving as you grow. He believes life is a continuous learning process, and the only way to succeed is to be open to new ideas and experiences. Branson's approach to life has allowed him to create multiple successful businesses across different industries, from music to airlines.

Branson started his career in the music industry, where he founded Virgin Records in 1972. Over the years, he expanded his business empire to include airlines, hotels, and even space tourism. Branson's approach to business is based on a simple principle: have fun and take risks. He believes that taking risks and embracing failure is essential to success. Branson is known for his adventurous spirit and willingness to take on new challenges. For example, in 2018, he completed a world-record-breaking swim across the English Channel at 68.

DOI: 10.4324/9781003364818-10

Another advocate of staying curious and evolving is Jeff Bezos, the founder of Amazon. Bezos is known for his customer-centric approach to business, which has allowed Amazon to become one of the most successful companies in the world. Bezos believes curiosity is critical to unlocking new opportunities and creating innovative solutions to complex problems. Bezos started Amazon in his garage in 1994 as an online bookstore. Over the years, Amazon expanded into other areas, such as music and electronics, and eventually became the world's largest online retailer.

One of the keys to Bezos' success has been his ability to embrace failure and learn from it. Bezos states, "I have made billions of dollars of failures at Amazon.com." For Bezos, failure is not something to be ashamed of; it's an essential part of the learning process. He encourages his employees to experiment, take risks, and learn from their mistakes.

Both Jeff Bezos and Richard Branson demonstrate that staying curious and evolving is not just a mindset but also a set of behaviors. They have taken risks and embraced failure as part of their learning process. They have both been willing to pivot their businesses and try new things. And perhaps most importantly, they have remained focused on their customers and employees, always seeking to innovate and improve their products and services. These leaders' approaches to life demonstrate that success is more than having it all figured out from the beginning. Instead, it's about being open to new experiences, embracing challenges, and evolving as you grow.

Staying curious doesn't mean that you have to be constantly on the move. It's about having an open mind and being willing to explore new ideas and perspectives. It's about being curious about the world around you and the people in it. When we are curious, we ask questions, seek answers, and explore new possibilities. We learn from our experiences and use them to shape our future.

Looking at it through the lens of the three C's, we can dig deeper into understanding how this state of being serves us in leadership. Since this lesson involves curiosity, let's start there. A friend of mine who is a therapist, coach, and self-love expert, Dr. Jane Tornatore, shared with me that we cannot be judgmental and curious simultaneously. I chewed on that statement for a long time. First, I tried to find instances where that could be untrue. And then, I began practicing being curious whenever I felt judgmental to see if I could maintain both states of being. It turns out she was right.

Traffic is where I find myself being the most judgmental. Why is this person in the passing lane? Why can't people merge correctly? Why is this person speeding while that person is going slow in the fast lane? When I noticed myself being judgmental about other people's driving habits, I started being curious instead. Maybe they are rushing to the hospital to see a critically ill family member. Perhaps they are sick themselves or dealing with some devastating news. On the other hand, it is possible that they could be from another country, and they are not used to our traffic laws and are super nervous about driving here. Do they really need an angry person honking at them to help them learn?

What happened was that I started realizing that judging people on one action wasn't fair and that practicing curiosity was a gateway to another C – compassion. So I found myself having compassion for these drivers. I don't understand their situation, so I shouldn't judge them for their actions.

As it relates to connection, we are all dealing with stuff, whether it shows up in traffic or other areas of life, and this is what connects us. Staying curious means being open to new experiences, different ways of thinking, and ideas you don't understand. Being on a journey doesn't mean sticking to a hard and fast pre-prescribed path. Instead, it means we are moving forward, and we stay open to whatever comes along.

This lesson includes stories of explorers on a voyage fueled by curiosity. Throughout their journeys, they evolved and adapted, ultimately creating lives and careers that are not only personally fulfilling but also have a lasting, positive impact on the world around them. As you read their stories, see if you can follow your curiosity to forge a path toward a life of continuous growth and meaningful achievements.

Steve Hoffman: A Curious Path From Hollywood to Tech Entrepreneur

Steve Hoffman, or Captain Hoff, as some refer to him, is most definitely a curious explorer. Steve started our conversation by saying he has had more careers than cats have had lives. Steve is the "Captain" and CEO of Founders Space, one of the world's leading startup accelerators, recognized by both Forbes and Entrepreneur as the number one incubator for overseas startups. Steve is also a venture investor and founder of three venture-backed and two bootstrapped startups. He is also the author of several award-winning books, including *Make Elephants Fly*, *Surviving a Startup*, and *The Five Forces*.

When I asked Steve about his career, he explained, "*I have been everything from an electrical engineer and game designer to a Hollywood TV development executive, voice actor, and manga writer. You name it, and I have done it.*" Steve says that it adds flavor to life. "*Some might say that's misdirected and confusing, but it keeps life interesting at the end of the day. I want a confusing life. I want to wake up and not know what I will be doing next year.*"

Steve's story began as a child with a passion for games. He loved role-playing and board games and computers and even learned how to code his own games. He also loved making movies, so Steve decided to go to film school. Steve's dad was a rocket scientist from MIT, and his mom was a crazy artist, he says he lucked out and got both of those genes.

Steve's rocket scientist father advised him, *"Son, nobody makes it in the film business. You should study computers. Computers are going to change the world."* This was a while back, and he was right. Steve took his dad's advice against his own judgment and shifted gears to study electrical computer engineering but found he wasn't passionate about it. Once he graduated, he decided to take the leap and do what he actually wanted to do.

He turned down job offers and instead went to the University of Southern California film school, and his life was never the same. Steve graduated from film school with a fantastic experience, but nobody handed him a job, just as his dad had predicted. He had plenty of great job offers in the electrical computer engineering field, but not a thing from film and television.

Steve got his hands on a copy of The Hollywood Directory, a guide with contact information for all the top TV executives in Hollywood. He brazenly sent off 150 printed letters to the top executives in Hollywood, hoping that someone would reply. With his Master's degree in hand, Steve was ready to go but had no prospects. Of the 150 letters, he ended up getting three replies. The first reply called Steve on the phone.

"Hello?" Steve answered. It was the producer of Star Wars: The Empire Strikes Back. He said, "I liked your letter. Unfortunately, I don't have a job for you, but I wanted to talk to you." They had an awkward conversation, with Steve's voice shaking the entire time. And that was that. But it was a bite! A conversation in the right field, at least!

The next call came from the head of development for Disney's Touchstone movie division at the time. She called Steve in for an interview, and it was going well; the typical back and forth when she then asked a trick question. "What movies do you like?"

Steve went to film school. He'd spent three years getting his Master of Fine Arts Degree, watching acclaimed artistic movies by Jean-Luc Godard, Federico Fellini, Francois Truffaut, and other obscure arthouse directors. He rattled off fantastic directors like Francis Ford Coppola and others he loved. She looked at Steve and said, "You didn't mention any Disney movies." Like a deer in headlights, Steve replied, "I loved Disney when I was a kid." Wrong answer. Her face dropped, and the interview was over. She couldn't wait to get him out of her office. Steve only had one last shot from the three responses he got.

Determined to prove his dad wrong, Steve resolved, *"I've got to make this work because nothing else is coming in. This is the only chance I have."*

Chuck Fries, who had a big office building across from the Mann's Chinese Theatre on Hollywood Boulevard with his name in big letters, called Steve into his office for an interview. At the time, Chuck had produced over 150 TV movies, mini-series, and projects. With the fresh interview fail with Disney on his mind, Steve knew what not to say.

"He called me into his office. I was not going to say I didn't watch television. I hadn't watched television in a while. I was in film school. There were all these great movies, but I'm not going to say that. I learned that lesson. I went into his office. He has this huge office with all these Emmys on the walls. He looked at me and said, 'Hoffman, I'm looking at your resume. You want a job.' I said, 'Yes. I want to write or direct films.' 'I don't know about that, Hoffman, but I'll see what I can do.'"

The next thing he knew, Steve got a job as a reader, meaning he would be paid a minuscule amount of money to read scripts. It sounded wonderful. Steve would get to read scripts and write up a synopsis – an opinion of the script and whether it should be produced. But the scripts can be pretty horrible. You're counted on, as a reader, to filter out the 99% of the bad scripts, tell them which are the good ones, and they'll read those. Readers are essentially giant filters. Even though he was dyslexic, making it extra challenging to read quickly, he powered through it and did as many scripts as they would give him.

After a couple of weeks, he was burnt out, and he didn't know how to get through to the head of the production company, so he sent a letter. In this letter, Steve wrote, "I can do more than this and offer you more. I went to film school." The reply came a week later, "Hoffman, it's only been a few weeks. How could you be unhappy with the job?" Steve replied, "I'm happy, but I could do more." Gruff silence followed, and then, "Hoffman, I don't know about this. Go away."

So Steve went away and waited. Sure enough, he got a promotion, and while he still had to be a reader, he got a job helping with a mini-series, doing research on The Oregon Trail about a character called Francis Parkman, one of the pioneers. Steve loved the research, dove into reading books, and wrote up a whole synopsis of the actual potential mini-series. Steve worked his butt off and did a great job, but he still felt like he wanted more.

The ever-persistent Steve sent another letter, which garnered the reply, "Hoffman! I gave you a promotion, and now you're asking for more? You have only been here a couple of months. Go away, Hoffman." So he did.

Then one day, Steve went into the office to pick up scripts to get back to reading because the research job was over. Steve walked into the head of development's office and asked, "Where are my scripts?"

The woman looked up at Steve, her eyes shooting daggers. She stood up and, through gritted teeth, said, "You got me fired." She picked up her stuff and stormed out of the office. Steve had no clue what was going on. A moment later, Chuck's assistant called Steve in, "Chuck wants to talk with you."

Once in the office, Chuck says, "Hoffman, you're my new head of development." Steve was confused. He didn't even ask for that job. Instead, he wanted to be a writer or director and didn't even know what a head of development actually did. Chuck broke the silence with, "Go back and do your job."

Walking into his new office with an out-of-place feeling, he looked out the window at the famous Mann's Chinese Theatre on Hollywood Boulevard and thought, *"This is bizarre. I don't know what this person does except hand me scripts. That's the only part of her job that I know."*

The phone rang, and although Steve didn't feel right answering it, he picked it up anyway. It was an agent from one of the big three agencies who wanted to talk about a project. That's when Steve realized he had to step into his new role with gusto, even if he had no idea what he was doing.

"I got called into Chuck's office the next day and didn't know what to do. I didn't know what she did besides handout scripts. They don't teach you this in film school. They show you art films, and you make some movies, but I wasn't making movies. I was in this business that I did not understand. I didn't watch any TV. I watched these art films for the past few years."

The next day Steve was sitting with Chuck and one of his sons, and they started talking about this TV movie that they were going to make.

"Chuck turns to me and says, 'Hoffman, you're the genius. Who should we put as the female lead?' I'm not one of these people who knows the names of actors or actresses, especially ones on TV unless they are super famous. I didn't know what to say. I think quickly and say, 'Chuck, let me get back to you on this.'

My brother's best friend was in Hollywood trying to make it. He has a photographic memory and is an encyclopedia of everything Hollywood, every little trivial thing. So I called him and said, 'Randy, we have this TV movie we're producing.' I described the part. I said, 'Who could do this?' He responded, 'That's easy. You could have this actress. She would be great' I'm writing down all these names I don't know.

The next day I go into Chuck's office. He says, 'Hoffman, did you think about it?' I said, 'Yes, Chuck. I did. This actress is my first choice. If she's not available, this actress, and if she's not available, try this one.' Chuck looked at me. 'Hoffman, you're a genius. Brilliant.'"

Steve fumbled his way through that job. But that was the beginning of his first career, where he learned the importance of persistence and showing up. He saw that you have to ask to get what you want and that sometimes it is okay to feel like an imposter when you are breaking into a new field.

Eventually, Steve realized he wasn't quite doing the creative work he desired while working in his current industry. It was time for a shift. He had heard of a mutual contact who founded the giant gaming company Sega in Japan. At the time, Sega had surpassed Nintendo to become the number-one video game company. He loved games and being creative, so he was eventually introduced to the company's Chairman and offered a job in Japan.

The next step was for Steve to stand before Chuck, quit his job, move to Japan, and make video games. Of course, Chuck thought Steve had lost his mind, leaving a promising career in Hollywood. He was right. It was crazy. "What are we going to do without you, Hoffman?" Chuck pondered. Steve suggested that Chuck hire his brother, who had no industry experience. Based on Steve's work to earn everyone's trust, his brother was hired, and Steve was off to Japan.

As I reflect on Steve's career, he is what I would call a great dot collector. He has had many different experiences throughout his career, and then he eventually found a way to connect the dots to see how they make sense.

In Japan, Steve was the only foreigner in the division; he was their token "gaijin" (foreigner), as they called him. His job was thinking up creative ideas, and his team produced mini-star tours, like a simulation ride, through outer space. The narrator and host for the ride was none other than Michael Jackson. He arrived at their offices and took people on a space tour. There were plans for rides to be built in Las Vegas and other places. Since Steve was an American, all the Japanese developers would pitch game ideas to him. They would say, "What do Americans think of this?" Whatever Steve's opinion was, that became the standard for what all Americans thought.

Sure enough, a year later, Steve remembered what his dad had told him when he started to hear about the internet coming in. It was just beginning to take off. He thought, *"I could make games myself. I don't have to work for this giant company doing games for them. I could do this. I have an engineering background. I have all these ideas."*

In another bold career move, Steve quit his job, returned to his home area, San Francisco, and launched his first company. That's how he became a tech entrepreneur, by coding his own games. He devised an idea to create non-violent games because he thought there were too many out there. His mission was simple, make them as fun as any shooter game out there and make them educational, but without feeling educational.

His first idea was a game called Gazillionaire, which is still available after all these years. Steve coded, did a lot of the artwork and drew it himself, and he enjoyed it because he got to be creative like he always wanted to be. After that, he started selling the game via mail order and making improvements along the way.

"Gazillionaire is a game that teaches people to be entrepreneurs. You run your own space trading company in outer space. It's supply and demand. You hire workers. They go on strike if you don't pay them well enough. You have

to decide whether to buy insurance. You have to purchase advertising, marketing dollars, and all this stuff in a fun, crazy outer space world.

I made the product with my own money. I bootstrapped it, but didn't know how to get it out there. I wasn't a game company or a publisher. There were these things called BBSs, Bulletin Board Systems, pre-internet.

I uploaded it to these bulletin boards where these geeks hang out to download shareware. They would download a trial version of the game, and if they liked it, then they would buy the full version. Sure enough, a week after I uploaded it because there was no eCommerce, I got $15 cash in the mail. I had the stack of floppy disks I shoved into a giant envelope and mailed it off to the person playing.

Orders started to trickle in. It wasn't enough to live off of, especially in the San Francisco Bay Area, but it was money. I heard that one of the largest PC game companies in the world at the time, Spectrum HoloByte MicroProse, their testers had downloaded my game and gotten hooked on it. It's an addictive game and fun. They wanted to put it out worldwide to every retail store everywhere.

The president called me up and said, 'Come on in. We want your game.' I'm negotiating with him for the game Gazillionaire. I suddenly figured out that this giant game company desperately needed my game. I'm like, 'Why does he need my game so much?' It turned out they let slip that their big production Star Trek, which they'd spent millions of millions of dollars on, was delayed and wouldn't launch until the next calendar year, yet they had to book revenue at the end of that year or their stock price would go down. They were a public company.

They gave me a significant advance on royalty. I couldn't believe it. I'd hit the jackpot with this little game. It went out there and did incredibly well. It got better reviews than their big multimillion-dollar production Star Trek, which pissed them off. The game was outdated the day I released it, but it was distinctive and funny. The graphics weren't pixel art, but they were like no other game out there, and people fell in love with it. That was my first entrepreneurial endeavor ever, and it was a fantastic experience."

Our conversation turned to his advice for entrepreneurs:

"There's no better way to make a product than if you are the customer and you are passionate about it because then you understand exactly what's in the customer's head. At the end of the day, you can always make your product better by talking to other people because they will see things, have perspectives, and have a way of experiencing your product that you can't have as the creator. There's no substitute for getting lots of feedback every step of the way. I was a complete nerd, so I was making products for other nerds.

One of the things I tell entrepreneurs is when you're starting your company, focus on something that people will be passionate about. It either has to solve a huge problem for them or provide a huge benefit to them, whether it's entertainment benefit, efficiency, or more money. Whatever the benefit is, it needs to be an enormous benefit."

Steve Hoffman's story is a testament to staying persistent and evolving. He has had many careers, and his success came from his ability to create products or work on projects that he would enjoy and constantly seek feedback to improve them. Steve's career trajectory is a reminder to stay curious and take risks, even if it means making unconventional career moves.

Hal Gregersen: Journey of Self-Discovery Through the Power of Questions

When you question yourself, you discover who you truly are. During our conversation, Hal Gregersen shared his childhood experience growing up with an abusive father. For most of his life, a shadow question always haunted him, "How can I make X happy?" However, it wasn't until he turned the shadow question he had hated for so long into a keystone question for himself that he found his true purpose.

Hal is a senior lecturer in leadership and innovation at MIT Sloan School of Management. He is also the former executive director of the MIT Leadership Center, a fellow at Innosight, and co-founder of the Innovators DNA consulting group. As an inspirational speaker, he has worked with renowned organizations such as Chanel, Disney, Patagonia, UNICEF, and the World Economic Forum. Thinkers50 recognized him as one of the world's most innovative minds. He has authored or co-authored 10 books translated into 15 different languages. Two of my favorites are *Questions Are the Answer: A Breakthrough Approach to Your Most Vexing Problems at Work and in Life* and *The Innovator's DNA: Mastering the Five Skills of Disruptive Innovators*.

Hal says that the flashpoints in his life, more often than not, were the moments when he got severely burned. It sounds like a strange starting point, but Hal's father was a construction worker, and his mother was a stay-at-home mom and sometimes an elementary school teacher. The family moved seven times before he was five years old as his father traveled to construction sites across the United States.

Imagine a family of five in a 30 × 8 × 8 feet tin can traveling across the country. The kids were full of energy, and looking back, Hal couldn't imagine how his parents dealt with it. While he had rich and fond memories of his childhood, he quickly learned that in their home, pretty much everything revolved around their father. It would be emotionally and sometimes physically abusive, and his father was the center of everything.

"If you didn't please him, sometimes it would become dangerous. So you learn fast how to make sure you do things, say things, and even think things that would calm down that dangerous force in your life and keep you safe.

All of that leads to me growing up with a very legitimate question for a four-year-old. How can I make this person happy so they don't hurt me in some way, shape, or form? When you're young and don't understand how the world works, that's a legitimate question. 'How can I make this dangerous adult happy?' When you grow up that way, all those memories get laid deep physiologically into your head. I didn't know it when I was younger and kept living with that question.

Instead of my father, it was, 'How can I make this teacher happy? How can I make my boss happy? How can I make my coworkers happy?' That question had its upside: an enormous commitment to working hard and trying to please other people by doing things and doing things with impact.

The downside is that it comes to a point where you are doing too much. As I unraveled that myself with colleagues and counselors over the years, the underlying question was, will I ever measure up and matter? When I say that out loud, it's still slightly embarrassing to this day, but it's life. It still holds its magnetic, attractive, and sometimes destructive energy if not conscious of it. So the question operates behind the scenes in my life."

When you are young, you are a sponge for everything around you; you absorb the good and the bad, and you learn what you need to do to survive and different coping mechanisms designed to keep you safe. For Hal, that meant becoming a people pleaser. Certain things don't ever go away. Of course, you recognize and manage them, but ultimately, it's more about embracing them and moving forward with them, especially as an adult.

Hal's life has been about a profound inner journey committing to understanding himself better to see what's underneath the covers. By opening up to the people around him and having them see him fully, he got help navigating the world in a different way.

"Many years ago, I was working with a group of leaders who were wrestling with gender equity in their organization. I had an insight about creating a sacred space where questions can emerge that will cause them to rethink and reflect, not just react, but recharge in a way that can take them in a different direction.

At that moment with that group, I said, 'Let's just stop and ask nothing but questions.' So we did, and at the end of ten minutes, when there were no answers, explanations, or questions, the energy level in the room went up. We reframed the issue and discussed ideas to move it forward. What miracle just happened here?

Many years later, I called it the question burst, and I use it often in my work. It could be one minute alone, just setting a timer and asking yourself questions, not answering questions and not explaining why, but asking nothing but questions. The data shows that individually or with people, we feel better 85% of the time and get at least one new idea. That's worth the few minutes.

The power of a question burst is that you can't respond. You've got to let it sit. There's that reflective, quiet space. Challenging questions can be such a gift."

Living a fulfilling life requires asking a lot of questions and embarking on an inner journey of self-discovery. This journey entails a commitment to understanding yourself at a deeper level and uncovering hidden aspects of yourself. Seeking the support of trusted friends and having honest conversations with them is also crucial. Vulnerability should not be feared as it holds immense power. By being open and receptive to receiving help and allowing others to see you in your entirety, they can guide you toward a new perspective on life. Only through this openness can they effectively assist you in navigating the world.

Hal believes that staying curious and evolving as you grow is essential. He shared how his passion for photography originated from his father's love for mechanical things and cameras. Growing up, he watched his father splicing film for his eight-millimeter movie camera. Hal's love for photography started when he received his first 35-millimeter camera from his parents after breaking his leg skiing when he was fifteen years old.

He developed his skills by buying a medium-format camera and even paid his way through college by working as a wedding and portrait photographer, capturing the essence of people through his lens. However, he stopped taking photographs after a traumatic experience of forgetting to pull out the dark slide (something older film cameras had to prevent light from coming through the lens and hitting the film) and ruining his friend's wedding photographs.

"It still hurts to say this to you, to hold the phone, and to tell him he has no wedding photos. It hurt so bad that over the course of the next five months, I stopped taking photographs. I didn't know how to deal with that kind of rejection, largely self-rejection."

After the tragic death of his first wife, Hal remarried, and his new wife encouraged him to rediscover his love for photography. He attended a workshop in Santa Fe, where he met Sam Abell, a National Geographic photographer, and Sam taught him to get dangerously close to people and see the world through a different lens. Sam advised putting down his telephoto lens (a long zoom) and choosing a wide-angle lens instead. As a result, Hal now uses photography to inform his research and gain more insight into various issues.

Hal has some words on his website that I think fundamentally sum up our conversation and the message that he shares in his various endeavors:

"When I look into the eyes of our grandchildren, I see pure wonder reflecting back. They're hungry with curiosity about the world around them, unafraid to explore, and eager to discover something new each day. We were all born with the gift of inquisitive creativity, something I believe we can sustain by the simple act of questioning.

I have dedicated my personal and professional life to this core questioning philosophy. We may not be able to turn back the hands of time to childhood. But if we never stop questioning, we never risk losing our own childlike sense of wonder and the power to disrupt the status quo."

Hal Gregersen's journey is a testament to the transformative power of questions and self-discovery. From his childhood experiences of abuse to his successful career as an author, speaker, and educator, Hal's willingness to question and explore his own thought patterns has enabled him to overcome personal and professional obstacles. Hal's work demonstrates the immense potential of asking questions to unlock our innate creativity, foster deeper connections, and ultimately lead more fulfilling lives. Through this commitment to the power of questions, we can rediscover our own childlike sense of wonder and, in doing so, continually evolve and grow.

Jeffrey Shaw: The Path to a Sustainable and Fulfilling Entrepreneurial Life

As entrepreneurs, we constantly change and evolve to get better at what we do and make a more significant contribution through our work. And that is definitely true for Jeffrey Shaw. Jeffrey can honestly say he never worked for anyone else. From selling eggs door to door at 14 years old, he began a lifetime of self-employment. As a speaker and small business consultant, Jeffrey guides self-employed and small business owners to gain control of their businesses. Jeffrey shows business owners how to see the business through a different lens. He is also the host of the top-rated podcast, The Self-Employed Life, and the author of *The Self-Employed Life: Business and Personal Development Strategies That Create Sustainable Success* and the fantastic *LINGO: Discover Your Ideal Customers Secret Language and Make Your Business Irresistible.*

One of the things about transformational tales is that it is simply our lives. We are living our lives, and it's only when somebody asks us to connect the dots that we can see them often because it's an iterative process. The transformational tales people will have to tell in the future, they likely don't see right now. So everybody's in a constant mode of adapting, changing, and evolving.

Jeffrey says, *"It comes down to other people finding our stories far more interesting than we do. We don't find our own journey unusual or particularly newsworthy, but people always ask, 'How did you go from being a photographer to what you do now?' It's the number one question I get asked. Is that unusual? I guess it is."*

When he said that, what popped into my head was the idea of slowing down to go fast. When you slow down and realize where you came from and all the things that have gotten you where you are, you can move forward in a more powerful way. It is recognizing that you must slow down and see those stories for what they are and how they can inform your path forward.

Jeffrey shares a flashpoint moment where he recalled the Sunday morning when he sat in the little garden at his Connecticut home in the Adirondack chair.

"I had been a full-time portrait photographer for very affluent families for years. I had a ridiculously good business. It was the easiest way to make money in the world. I loved what I did at every moment, and I got to be creative.

I photograph entirely on locations. I'm outside. My clients all have multiple homes, so they flew me all over the world. It's ridiculous how good it was. Here I was, many years in, reaping the benefits and rewards of this remarkable photography career and having this nagging feeling that there had to be more for me. I felt like I have to contribute something more to the world.

What more can I offer the world? On the side, I started receiving some training as a coach. I remember thinking to myself. I felt like I'm having an affair with myself. It was this weird way that I didn't want my photography clients to know I was interested in doing something else. Why? Because we've always been told we have to focus on one thing. We've been told we have to pick a niche in business. I had a very niche business serving a very demanding clientele. I didn't want them to think that if I was doing something else, I couldn't be as good for them because that's what I've been told my whole life.

We have always been told that classic phrase, 'Jack of all trades, master of none,' which is my biggest pet peeve in life. Who decided we can only be good at one thing? I've since learned to compare this to love. I have three kids. I loved my first child immensely when he was born. Did I not have as much love for the second and third child? Of course, not. Because your love capacity expands to include what needs to fit into it, why can't our talents and skill sets?

That was a significant flashpoint moment in my life where I permitted myself to be true to who I am as a business person. As it turns out, all those years later, that's the number one piece of advice I give, and what I do for my coaching clients every day is to help them build a business model of multiples, where they are making multiple income streams and serving various audiences. Because not only is it what sustains you and keeps you excited about your business every day, but it's also the smartest business model."

That Sunday morning, Jeffrey was battling this inner turmoil. He had two websites going, one for his photography business and one for his coaching practice, and he felt like he was hiding the fact that he was running two businesses at one time. So that Sunday morning, he got up from that Adirondack chair, walked into his office, and combined his photography and coaching websites into one domain.

"I am one person, a whole person, and I happen to be somebody who photographs, runs a business, wants to help other people run their business, and wants to be a coach. I am one person, and I am tired of living in a way that people tell me I should fragment myself and hide one piece for myself for another."

His instinct was right. That set the ball in motion for Jeffrey to diversify, cross-market, and combine his talents. So many of us see ourselves as specialists in one area. However, we contain multitudes. When we hold ourselves back from being the things that we could and should be, then what we are doing is we are holding ourselves back from our full potential. It's great to have people like Jeffrey who help people see more of themselves.

Jeffrey recalls struggling for the first three years of his photography business. He was only 20 years old, married, had an apartment, and had several financial commitments. At that point, the scariest thing to him was the fear of having a failing business at 23 years old, and photography was the only thing he knew. *"This was a talent I had that I felt I could excel at, but this is all I had, so if this didn't work, I was screwed. There was pressure because I didn't know anything else."* Jeffrey became self-employed because he deemed himself to be entirely unemployable. He saw himself as shy, a geek, and a nerd.

"If you had asked me 12 years ago why I thought I was on this Earth, I would have said to be a photographer. Ask me that now and I have a very different answer."

Since *The Virtual Campfire* was created during the global pandemic, many conversations were around how people used that experience as a transition point.

"When the pandemic hit, I was at a good point. I felt very grounded on where I was going, and I was just beginning to write my book, The Self-Employed Life. So I made it a rule for myself, which I've continued to stick with: whenever somebody came to mind, I would reach out to them because I assumed there had to be a reason somebody came to mind."

Jeffrey began reaching out to those who popped into his mind to let them know he could support them. The pandemic had brought challenges to so many of us, and he felt that based on his own life experiences, he could be a reservoir of hope or energy to someone who needed it.

"This was my third rodeo. I'd been through 9/11 as a New Yorker and survived the Great Recession serving the affluent people that were the ones on the news. That reduced my business by 2/3 in a year.

I knew we were in for at least a year-long trauma when this came along. It went on a bit longer than I estimated because of my mindset. All those things contributed to feeling like I had this reservoir of well-being and knowing not everybody will find themselves in that position and why not share what I had to give when I had that capacity. My book, The Self-Employed Life, is an unusual business book because there is so much coaching and a focus on personal development. People have asked me, 'Why is there so much personal development? It's such an unusual approach to a business book.'

I say, 'Because I'm tired of a world where people are given strategies and how-tos without focusing on the personal development capacity to handle all the hard work.' It's the number one stopping block. You can keep working hard, putting in all the hours, and you wonder, 'How come I'm not getting any place?' Here's why personal development is essential. It comes down to capacity. You have to increase the capacity of what you're capable of, what you believe you deserve, and what you see yourself as deserving. You have to increase that capacity in order for the hard work and strategy to go somewhere.

Expectation, by definition, is a predetermined outcome. You have already decided on the limitations of your success. Subconsciously or not, you have already determined it. Often, other people can see more in us than we can see in ourselves."

Watching award shows like the Grammys, in those speeches, everybody always thanks other people. They always thank the people who believed in them more than they believed in themselves. So the best way for us to be bigger than we are is to see what other people see in us and start believing them.

Jeffrey recalls. *"I encourage everyone to just look at themselves holistically. I did a tremendous amount of work around my core values over the past couple of years. My number one core value is acceptance. To me, acceptance is way beyond diversification and accepting people of all races, genders, and orientations. It is about accepting the uniqueness of who we are."*

Acceptance comes down to knowing that the answers are within. You have to trust yourself to know the answers are there. Once you accept, you can transcend that limitation and get there. The secret to success, Jeffrey believes, is finding the sweet spot in what seems to be polar opposites. *"To me, business is being soulful and being strategically smart."*

Jeffrey Shaw's entrepreneurial journey shows the power of embracing our multitudes and transcending limitations. He has paved the way for a more sustainable and fulfilling business model that harnesses our diverse talents and passions by challenging the notion that we must focus on a single niche. Through his work, he emphasizes the importance of personal development and self-acceptance, helping others to expand their capacity for success and to see themselves as deserving of it. In the ever-evolving world of entrepreneurship, Jeffrey's story is an inspiring reminder that we are not confined to a single path or identity. By slowing down and recognizing our unique stories, we can propel ourselves forward with renewed purpose and passion, ultimately achieving greater heights in both business and life.

The Lessons

Through their diverse experiences, these life explorers have embraced vulnerability, persistence, and adaptability. They have also demonstrated how connecting the dots between various experiences, passions, and skills can lead to personal and professional growth, innovation, and success. As we navigate life's complex and ever-changing landscape, these stories remind us that no experience is wasted. Instead, we can foster a well-rounded, fulfilling, and impactful life by seeking new opportunities and perspectives.

Steve Hoffman had multiple careers, from electrical engineering to Hollywood TV development and authoring award-winning books. Persistence, showing up, and asking for what we want is critical in breaking into new fields and overcoming imposter syndrome. Steve's journey from film school to game development to founding a tech startup demonstrates that creating products or services that resonate with your target audience and provide significant value can lead to success. Ultimately, Steve's story highlights the importance of embracing a diverse, interesting, and sometimes confusing life to ensure continuous growth and evolution.

Despite facing challenges in his early life, Hal Gregersen managed to develop his innate curiosity and evolve. His love for photography, which originated from his father's passion for mechanical things and cameras, played a significant role in his personal and professional growth. Through self-discovery and seeking support from trusted friends, Gregersen highlights the importance of staying true to oneself, embracing vulnerability, and converging art, business, and science. It's never too late to rediscover a lost passion and find new ways to integrate it into your life.

Jeffrey Shaw's transformation from a renowned portrait photographer to a small business coach highlights the importance of staying curious and evolving as we grow. Embracing multiple talents and skill sets, Jeffrey encourages diversification and cross-marketing in order to sustain and maintain excitement in our businesses. The secret to success lies in finding the intersection of deep personal meaning and marketability, fostering a well-balanced ecosystem through personal development, right-sized business strategies, daily habits, and mindsets. By accepting and trusting ourselves and combining soulfulness with strategic smarts, we can navigate a powerful and fulfilling journey in life and business.

Questions

As we wrap up Lesson 9, let's circle back to the three C's of grounded leadership: curiosity, compassion, and connection, with some questions for you to ponder and journal.

- How do you typically approach new opportunities or challenges? Are you hesitant, or do you embrace them with curiosity and openness?
- What are some areas in your life where you would like to cultivate more curiosity? What steps can you take to foster a greater sense of wonder and exploration in those areas?
- Reflect on a time when you resisted change or growth. What held you back, and how can you use curiosity to overcome similar obstacles in the future?
- Have you ever pursued a passion that turned out not to be what you expected? How did you pivot and evolve from that experience?

End Notes

"I have made billions of dollars of failures at Amazon.com." More Amazon Fire Phones Are Coming, Jeff Bezos Signals. *Vox*, December 2, 2014

The Hollywood Directory. Hollywood Creative Directory Staff. Hollywood Creative Directory. Edited by Cary Tusan and L. M. Siegel, Hollywood Creative Directory, 2008

Gazillionaire Game. Spectrum Holobyte, 1994

Make Elephants Fly – Steve Hoffman

Surviving a Startup – Steve Hoffman

The Five Forces – Steve Hoffman

Questions Are the Answer – Hal Gregersen

The Innovator's DNA – Hal Gregersen

The Self-Employed Life – Jeffrey Shaw

LINGO – Jeffrey Shaw

Don't Go It Alone

Being an entrepreneur or starting something new can feel lonely. It's easy to get lost in your own self-doubts, but the truth is most successful initiatives come from people working together. Even when something impressive is accomplished, people often realize they didn't do it alone – they had the support of a network of people along their journey. In this lesson, we will explore the importance of connecting with others, not being afraid to ask for help, realizing the power in numbers, and leveraging the complementary strengths of others.

When I think about accomplishing something big in the world together, my thoughts often go back to the Renaissance. It was an expansive period that is considered a time of outstanding artistic, scientific, and intellectual achievement, and it profoundly impacted the development of Western culture. This period was also known for collaboration and collective thinking, where artists came together to support, inspire, and raise each other's contributions to the world. Historians think of it as an incubator for some of history's most significant artistic accomplishments. Today, you don't have to be a painter, a sculptor, or a musician to be part of a Renaissance. Having a mission to make a positive impact through your work is enough to get you into the club.

The synergy between people working together is a powerful force. When we connect with the people who believe in and support us, we open ourselves up to new possibilities. In his book, *Give and Take*, organizational psychologist Adam Grant argues that success is not just about individual talent and hard work. It's also about the power of relationships and the support we receive from others. For example, seeking out a mentor, joining a networking group, or attending a conference can be great ways to connect with others and build a supportive community.

We also have to get comfortable with asking for help. It can be difficult, but it's an essential part of the journey to success. Asking for help is not a sign of weakness, but a sign of strength. It shows that you're willing to be vulnerable and that you value the input of others.

DOI: 10.4324/9781003364818-11

We all have different strengths and weaknesses. Leveraging the complementary strengths of others can be a powerful way to achieve success. In his book, *Good to Great*, management consultant Jim Collins argues that great teams are not made up of individual superstars but of individuals who work well together and complement each other's strengths. Whether it is partnering with someone with different skills or expertise, collaborating on a project with someone with a different perspective, or joining forces with others to achieve a common goal, you need to leverage the strengths of others. When we collaborate, we build upon each other's strengths and create something greater than we could on our own. Jazz music provides a great example of collaboration. Jazz musicians work off each other, improvising and building on each other's ideas to create something unique and beautiful.

Don't go it alone. The journey to success is not a solo one. By connecting with others, asking for help, realizing the power in numbers, and leveraging the complementary strengths of others, you can achieve greater success and fulfillment. In this lesson, we will explore how the power of collaboration and a supportive network can amplify your impact on the world.

Don't get me wrong, it is not always easy when a group of people comes together. Conflicts arise, and relationships get tested; however, these instances are also filled with valuable lessons. We can learn to navigate collaborations that work well and how to manage healthy conflict. You will read some powerful stories of people who have joined forces to create a meaningful impact through their combined efforts and how you can leverage these lessons in your own partnerships and teams.

Jen Guillemin and Wendy Swart Grossman: A Harmonious Collaboration at the Intersection of Art and Business

What do business and the arts have in common? Some might say nothing, but the co-founders of Creative Re/Frame, Jen Guillemin and Wendy Swart Grossman, have a different answer. They recognize that business needs art, and art needs business. Their mission is to bring the two together to create a powerful and balanced world for both.

Wendy is a creative practitioner and consultant with a background in the United States and South African Presidential campaigns. She brings her expertise in building effective partnerships, strategic planning, board development, communication, and facilitation to everything she does. Wendy has held positions at the Harvard Museum of Science and Culture and the Graduate School of Design. She has also worked with the Science Museum in London and scores of NGOs, non-profits, and social impact businesses nationally and internationally. She is also an Adjunct Faculty member at Boston University within the Graduate Arts Administration Program.

Jen is an arts advocate and creative problem-solver. She has taught and mentored art and design students at Northeastern University in their world-renowned Co-op Program. Many organizations have sought her expertise in higher education administration, building effective partnerships, strategic visioning, curriculum development, and cross-sector collaboration. Her professional affiliations have led her to teach in prisons and homeless shelters to create community-engaged projects. Jen's passion is to help people identify and focus on personal values, creative interests, and unique gifts to achieve their educational, professional, and personal goals.

So what brought these two individuals together? As mentioned, Wendy and Jen co-founded Creative Re/Frame, a consulting practice integrating the arts in entrepreneurship and innovation spaces on university campuses. They are a remarkable duo who can create a huge impact by working together.

Wendy has been a traveler since childhood, living in various places before age 12. This led her to search for community and connection wherever she went. Wendy continued to move around, living out of a backpack for six months and working as an organizer for different causes and political campaigns. She was curious about what compelled people to get involved in politics and purpose.

Wendy's career evolved, starting with organizing for regional political groups in Steubenville, Ohio. She was also a student organizer at UMass Amherst and Bridgewater State, canvassing to make ends meet. In addition, she worked at paper mills during shift breaks in Stevens Point, Wisconsin, and was interested in learning about people's motivations for getting involved in politics. She searched for community and connection throughout her journey, and these experiences have shaped her worldview.

Jen grew up in upstate New York in a stable home filled with music, a house her dad still lives in today. Her mom was a voice teacher at a nearby college, and she also had private students. Jen remembers her mom using music to help people find joy and express their emotions. Her home always seemed to have a way of leaving people with joyful feelings after they visited. Sadly, Jen's mom passed away from cancer, and it became clear to her that the community her mom had was precious. She had endless gifts delivered and visitors around in the days leading up to her passing. After hearing some of their stories and seeing the impact her mom's music had on others, she knew there was an intersection between relationships and the arts.

Shortly after arriving in Boston, Jen met Sidewalk Sam, who eventually became her father-in-law. Sidewalk Sam was well known for his public artwork, which drew people together. The opportunity to witness the magic of what it takes to bring people together and experience the arts is what helped Jen define her career direction. After earning her Master's in Arts Administration, she pursued a Master's in Counseling.

Jen noticed that her students had exceptional talents and abilities but needed to prepare for a life in the arts.

"Through these years of working with students, I found that they had these amazing talents and abilities, but we needed to do something to help prepare them for a life in the arts. When they graduated, they didn't even have a resume. They needed to understand how they might continue to lead a creative life in the arts.

I cared deeply about this, mostly because I cared about the people and the community. I was invested. I started experimenting with offering various programs for students to gain skills. At this time, I met my fabulous colleague, friend, collaborator, and amplifier of all that is good, Wendy Swart Grossman.

I was sharing the work with her. She also had an interest in teaching. I taught a class in Arts Administration, and the head of the department invited me to propose a course. Initially, we thought it would be an interesting combination of our skills where we would have artists as activists. So we created a proposed curriculum.

We went and chatted with the director of the program. He brought to light that there was this whole new thing popping up on how can we morph this into cultural entrepreneurship, which was mind-blowing at the time for us, but it gave us a much more concrete series of things that we could hang our combined skill sets onto from Jen's incredible knowledge of the whole art world and my get-things-done mentality."

Their course continues to be filled to capacity every semester and is still running.

According to Jen, *"We found that we would start someplace, but by combining skills, we could always improve things. I would say something, and Wendy would build off it. We knew we could go much further by working together. We started to see what we were teaching, the quality of the teaching, what we were able to produce in our writing, how we were able to support our students, and it would grow so we would come up with an idea and it made fun to be able to do this. We have created something and are seeing demand for what we're creating. So let's start Creative Re/Frame."* *And that is precisely what they did."*

During their years working together, it became clear that 1+1 did not just equal 2 in Wendy and Jen's case. They were vastly different individuals, but together, they complimented each other so well that they found the success they were looking for while pursuing their passions and supporting others.

Wendy says that. *"Jen is the kind of person who, when you're talking to her, she's looking at your soul. You would think you're the most important person in the world. She asks you questions like, 'How's your spirit? How would you be best fulfilled?' The way Jen moves in the world was like a bomb to the soul."*

Like any partnership, they have had their differences but *"place a high value on harmony. When things are a little off, we initially give each other a little space but always discuss and address it. That has been such a gift because I know I can be honest. I always feel safe in honesty and trust that whatever has happened, we both have a shared commitment to getting back to our harmonious place because that's where we can do our best work."*

In the early stages of creating Creative Re/Frame, they talked about making like an artist, caring like an activist, strategizing like an entrepreneur, and implementing like an organizer. Jen and Wendy agree, *"The time has come for us to stop pretending that we can live in a world devoid of our expressive selves. We have teased businesses apart from what it means to be human. Fundamentally, people are not happy working in their current environments. Working in environments devoid of human connection does not feel meaningful to people. But, we also see that living in a time when we are not factoring in people is not sustainable. That time is over for us. Creative Re/Frame is the answer to that and will focus on supporting others to access their creative selves so they can be their best selves."*

We see the potential for the arts to open up those conversations and connections.

"We're only beginning to ignite our imagination about where this could go. We see so much possibility. We aim to work with universities because we see them as a way to educate people and open up their imaginations. Don't be afraid of people who are different because that's where the conversation gets fascinating."

Jen Guillemin and Wendy Swart Grossman's ability to combine their skill sets has led to a transformative and impactful relationship. They have combined their entrepreneurship, innovation, and creative expertise to create a consulting practice that bridges the gap between the two worlds. By sharing their experiences and professional backgrounds, their passion for community, connection, and personal growth through the arts has become a foundation for everything they do together. Wendy and Jen's successful partnership is a testament to the power of collaboration and complementary skills. They have built a program that inspires and empowers others to tap into their creative selves and make a meaningful impact.

Michael Hendrix and Panos Panay: A Musical Approach to Collaboration and Creativity

Collaboration and creativity can create strange yet wonderful partnerships that produce great art. And there are business lessons to be learned from these partnerships. Michael Hendrix and Panos Panay are inspiring collaborators who are entrepreneurs, musicians, and co-authors of *Two Beats Ahead: What Musical Minds Teach Us About Innovation*. I was immediately drawn to their book because I love exploring ideas from different perspectives. *Two Beats Ahead* explores the similarities between music and innovation, highlighting the importance of collaboration, diversity, experimentation, and learning from failure. Panos and Michael are the perfect guides for this journey.

Michael is a Partner and Global Design Director at IDEO and an Assistant Professor of Music, Business, and Management at Berklee College of Music. He has had an impressive design portfolio working on everything from home goods to homeland security and everything in between. He is also the co-founder of the Open Music Initiative.

Panos is the Co-President of The Recording Academy and a Fellow at MIT Connection Science. He founded Sonicbids, a platform for bands to book gigs and market themselves online, and co-founded the Open Music Initiative with Michael.

Panos' story begins in Nicosia, Cyprus, where his first musical memory was watching Elvis Presley in the movie, "King Creole." He was immediately amazed by the baseline and vocal performance. He credits this specific moment in history with starting his lifelong quest of wanting to be in the music world. As a result, he applied to Berklee College of Music without a plan B. He loved the music business and became a talent agent for many artists he admired growing up. Through that experience, he began his company Sonicbids, and after 13 years, he sold it and founded the Institute for Creative Entrepreneurship (ICE) at Berklee. Over time, his journey took him to be in charge of the overall institutional strategy for Berklee.

Michael's story is slightly different. He doesn't recall a time in his life when there wasn't music. His dad loved to sing and was always involved in choir or singing in church. His mom played both the organ and the piano. His venture into music began with piano lessons that he didn't love at a young age, eventually leading him to the acoustic guitar. While he loved playing music, he never thought it would relate to his career.

Michael went on to take design, and only a few years ago, after meeting Panos, he started thinking about how he could use design to improve music. So it was time to explore.

Michael and Panos met at an innovation conference, and their conversation centered around what music can do in design and vice versa. Their conversation ended up creating the "weaving of those two worlds."

Panos recalls, *"I remember getting an email from Michael in my inbox. The email you get when you meet somebody is always like, 'It was great meeting you ... .' It's always fascinating because how many emails do we get that we missed or failed to respond to because our inbox is so full? I always feel you meet people, get a business card, return to your office, and usually end it there. The difference between picking it up and sending somebody a thank you note or leaving it there can change the trajectory of your life forever."*

Michael and Panos came together with different skill sets and no formal intention of creating something together. Instead, it was based on mutual respect and interest and supporting each other. Michael states, *"A good relationship is not interested in keeping score. It is about what could be possible. Panos and I worked together because we've always been interested in what can be. In our book, we talk about collaboration and collaborative relationships. It's not one of us having an agenda or setting the vision for the other and asking the other to follow along. It's more about two people, shared collaborators, coming together to make something. There's a point at which you don't know who's responsible for what. That's perfect because something new emerges from that."*

Their partnership has grown simply through trust and collaboration. It reminds me of jazz-style improvisation. They throw this beat down, or this note, and the next person picks up, and off they go. There's not a clear plan as to what they want to create. The options are open. It starts with someone having the passion and the courage to make that first move. Then the other person is willing to work with that.

With any partnership, there are always challenges. For Michael and Panos, co-authoring a book was a challenge. Panos remembers, *"The agents had originally approached Michael to write a book. Michael said, 'I don't have time, but talk to my friend Panos.' I'm this sucker who says yes to everything. So I started writing the book. I'm like, 'I can't do this on my own. It will be so much more fun if Michael comes on board. We would geek out together about all these musical joys we share.' During the three years of writing, we had multiple false starts and times when I got frustrated and shut down. I couldn't write, and there were times when Michael got frustrated. There were many points where either of us, or sometimes both of us, decided we should walk away. We asked for an extension from our publisher. We were like the temperamental rockstar who goes into a studio and spends too much money trying to perfect the drum sound."*

Michael recounts, *"Creativity is hard, especially to be good at it. It's not hard to come up with a lot of ideas, but it's hard to get them to good ideas and then to great ones. We use a Justin Timberlake quote, 'Dare to suck,' which is this idea that you will be vulnerable enough to share ideas early. You do that because you want other people to be able to respond to them, hear your intention and then build on that idea. It's the 'Yes-And' concept. We have those moments where if you embrace it as an iterative process and you are like, 'This thing didn't work,' but it made you pivot to this direction, and now you have got something new, then you pivot again. It's still painful and hard, but it is not a blow to your ego. You are not saying, 'I failed.'"*

Michael and Panos are a true testament to bringing the best out in each other. As individuals, they are very different. Michael is introverted, and Panos is extroverted. Michael is from the United States, and Panos is from Cyprus. Their common ground is their passion for music, and their collaborations have been successful partly because of their differences.

They believe that their differences play an essential role in the success of their collaborations. They also have a *"loose shared purpose that's been good for us. We haven't had to define that so tightly that we're either in or out of it. That can be a huge contributor to whether people choose to continue to work together or not. You have to have that kind of optimism that something good will happen. It's not well-defined but amorphous enough that the belief in the outcome is what motivates you. Not a definition of the outcome."*

When working on their book, they wanted to remind people, *"We should not see creative education as one that is purely meant to be practically applied by somebody becoming a performer. Instead, it awakens the spirit and the mind and enables you to see possibilities that are unseen by most people.*

There is a reason why most Nobel laureates also tend to have an artistic background in addition to their main discipline; a minor to their major. That minor tends to be a creative pursuit. That was their ambition behind 'Two Beats Ahead.' It is intended to introduce a question: Can we or should we be looking at today's problems using a different framework? Our existing systems or existing frameworks of organizing our companies, our governments, and how we manage people, do they still apply, or is it time for us to rethink them? We argue that it's time to rethink them. As Tim Cook said in an address to MIT graduates several years ago, I'm paraphrasing here, but he said something like, 'I'm less worried about robots thinking like humans. I'm more worried about humans thinking like robots.'"

The collaboration between Michael Hendrix and Panos Panay exemplifies how creative partnerships can lead to great art and innovation. Their partnership is a true testament to bringing out the best in each other, despite their differences in personality and background. They focus their collaboration on the belief that something positive will emerge from their projects together and aim to inspire others to see possibilities that are unseen by most people. And their book challenges readers to rethink existing frameworks and encourages creativity in problem-solving. Overall, their story is a reminder that the power of collaboration and creativity can lead to unexpected but beautiful outcomes.

The Lessons

Entrepreneurship doesn't have to be a lonely journey. Getting caught up in the idea that we must do everything alone is easy, but that's not the case. Instead, we need to connect with others who believe in our work and support us fully. Through these connections, we can create a powerful network of support that can help us achieve our goals.

Jen Guillemin and Wendy Swart Grossman recognize that business needs art, and art needs business. They have built a consulting practice integrating the arts in entrepreneurship and innovation spaces on university campuses. By combining their skills and expertise in entrepreneurship, innovation, and the arts, Jen and Wendy have built a successful partnership that inspires and empowers others to tap into their creative selves and make a meaningful impact. Their partnership is a testament to the power of collaboration and complementary skills. It shows the importance of embracing our expressive selves and bringing more humanity into our work environments.

Michael Hendrix and Panos Panay's collaboration as entrepreneurs, musicians, and co-authors highlights the importance of collaboration, diversity, experimentation, and learning from failure. Despite their different backgrounds and personalities, their creative partnership exemplifies how working together can lead to great art and innovation. Their book challenges readers to rethink existing frameworks and encourages creativity in problem-solving. Their story is a testament to the power of collaboration and creativity in producing unexpected but beautiful outcomes.

So, as you move forward on your entrepreneurial journey, remember that you don't have to go it alone. Connect with others, make music together, and embrace the power of collaboration. With the right support system in place, there's no limit to what you can achieve.

Questions

As we wrap up this lesson, let's circle back to the three C's of grounded leadership: curiosity, compassion, and connection, with some questions for you to ponder and journal.

- Have you ever felt like you had to go it alone in your entrepreneurial journey? How has that affected your progress and success?
- Who are the people in your life that believe in your work and support you fully? How can you strengthen those connections to build a more powerful support network?
- How can you tap into your creativity to approach collaborations with an open mind and combine skill sets with others?

- Can you think of a time when collaboration with others led to unexpected and amazing results? What made that collaboration successful?

End Notes

Tim Cook to MIT Grads: "How Will You Serve Humanity?" Chandler, David L. MIT News, June 9, 2017, Accessed June 19, 2023
   Give and Take – Adam Grant
   Good to Great – Jim Collins
   Two Beats Ahead – Michael Hendrix and Panos Panay

Conclusion

Divergent Minds, Convergent Hearts

When I committed to being an entrepreneur, I mainly worked independently and started to crave connection with others. I didn't just want to be around other people; I really wanted to have a deeper connection with others, something that felt meaningful. This led me to the idea of bringing people together and sharing their stories with others. I never imagined it would become a podcast. If you had told me back then I would ever host a podcast, I would have told you that you were crazy. I didn't know much about podcasting, but in the face of a global pandemic and craving community, I plunged into the unknown.

The original concept was getting people together to share their stories in an intimate setting. I would call it "Divergent Minds, Convergent Hearts," which was about people who think differently coming together, sharing their thoughts and stories, and leaving connected as one community. But, as many of the best-laid plans do, my original idea morphed into something totally different and unexpectedly beautiful.

As much as I had given thought to my idea, this sharing of great minds and connecting of indomitable spirits, I didn't understand how much it would impact me. Hearing these inspiring stories from so many people I admired gave me insights into wisdom that I had never considered or only had small glimpses of in my life journey.

This book has featured only a few of my incredible guests. I have been fortunate to sit down with some of the greatest minds of our modern day (and I am just getting started). It's so easy to put people up on a pedestal and assume they have the perfect mix of talents, gifts, and luck for their lives to lead to such success. We might imagine their lives have not been fraught with struggle, sacrifice, or imposter syndrome. We may see them as naturally courageous, clever, socially agile, and well-connected. Through these many conversations, I have come to understand that everyone has a story. Their journeys have led them through many situations in which they made tough choices, learned hard lessons, navigated through challenging

DOI: 10.4324/9781003364818-12

dilemmas, and came out on the other side with wisdom, compassion, and a heart generous enough to share their hard-won experiences.

There are many lessons to be learned from great leaders, artists, creative thinkers, and idea generators. My hope in writing this book was not only to share the wisdom of these beautiful conversations but also to offer a challenge to you as the reader:

- How can you use these lessons and ideas to influence your own style of self-leadership and leading others?
- What lessons have you learned in your own journey?
- What are your personal flashpoints, and how have they changed the course of your life?
- What communities can you plug into, and who can you connect with to form your own campfire circle?
- What lessons would you hand down to others?

In my quest to share the message of grounded leadership, I want to offer some parting advice of my own. Whether you are leading yourself, a team, or an entire organization, a time will come when you will be asked to make a quick decision or address an important issue. If staying grounded during calm times is a practice, staying grounded during times of crisis is a form of art. Just like building any muscle, the key is repetition. We must stretch our capabilities and shift our thinking to face new challenges gracefully.

As you move forward from this book, I encourage you to create spaces of your own for connection and build your communities. Many of us can often find ourselves in echo chambers, surrounded by voices that sound much like our own. While connection can undoubtedly be found there, we might find that we lack the growth that comes with expanding our circle to include voices from different industries, parts of the world, and backgrounds and therefore miss out on all the wisdom that comes with those people.

You can create a world where diverse voices converge, conversations flow freely, and bonds are forged across differences. By forming our own communities, we invite a vibrant mosaic of experiences and perspectives to weave together. We can embrace the opportunity to engage in heartfelt conversations to enrich our understanding, broaden our horizons, and build bridges. There is so much beauty in making space for these unique stories to unfold. Together, we can create a wondrous journey of forging meaningful connections through honest conversations, nurturing our collective growth, and embracing the beauty of our shared humanity.

Index

Printed in the United States
by Baker & Taylor Publisher Services